Psychic Ancestry

Psychic Ancestry
A Magical Link to the Past
Using Unconventional Methods

Terri Blair

STANDING
STONES
PRESS

Standing Stones Press
Milwaukee, Wisconsin
sstonespress@icloud.com
www.terriblairauthor.com

Psychic Ancestry: A Magical Link to the Past Using Unconventional Methods

Copyright © 2024 by Terri Blair.

All rights reserved. No part of this book may be used or reproduced, distributed or transmitted in any form or by any means, including photocopying, recording or other electronic or mechanical methods, without the prior written permission from the owner/author.

Ancestry trademarks, logos, and brand names are and remain the property of Ancestry and its affiliated entities. I am not—nor are these materials—sponsored, affiliated, endorsed, or otherwise associated with or by Ancestry and its affiliated entities, and use of their trademarks, logos, or brand names is for informational purposes only and does not imply any support or endorsement by Ancestry or its affiliated entities.

First Edition
First Printing, 2025
ISBN Paperback: 979-8-218-57780-3
ISBN eBook: 979-8-218-58789-5

Interior pages design by Creative Publishing Book Design
Cover design by Ellen Bednarek Design
Cover images:
    Labyrinth-Ruslan Batiuk | Dreamstime.com
    Tree-Vasiltigaj | Dreamstime.com
    Silhouette-Bins28 | Dreamstime.com
    Silhouettes- Tankas | Dreamstime.com
    Silhouette-Mst Lipi Begum | Dreamstime.com

Printed in the U.S.A.

CONTENTS

Part One
PSYCHIC RESEARCH BEGINS

Chapter 1
Mysteries to Solve, 3

Chapter 2
The Search for Annie's Real Father, 7

Chapter 3
My Mother as Ancestor, 15

Chapter 4
A Psychic Journey, 21

Part Two
THE CLANS
(MCINTOSH, COUPER, BLAIR & MATHIESON)

Chapter 5
The Highland Women, 35

Chapter 6
A Mysterious Photo Appears, 47

Chapter 7
The Disappearance of Thomas Couper, 57

Chapter 8
The Coupers in America, 67

Chapter 9
Poorhouse Alexandrina, 77

Chapter 10
Stories of the Blairs, 89

Part Three
SPOOK HILL: WONEWOC SPIRITUALIST CAMP & WILLIAM SANTAS

Chapter 11
Spook Hill: William Santas, 99

Chapter 12
Wonewoc Mediumship Class, 107

Part Four
MY POLISH ANCESTORS

Chapter 13
The Skis as Ancestors, 119

Chapter 14
Circumstantial Evidence, 129

Part Five
PSYCHIC KIN, PROTECTION & SPIRIT GUIDES

Chapter 15
In Search of Psychic Kin, 139

Chapter 16
Protection, 149

Chapter 17
Spirit Guides & Guardian Angels, 155

Part Six
HOW I DID IT & EPILOGUE

Chapter 18
How I Did It & Sometimes Things Just Show Up, 167

Epilogue, 177

Resources, 179

FAMILY TREES

The McIntosh Family, 6

The Highland Women, 34

Frederick Couper's Family, 46

The Sea Captains (Coupers), 56

Poorhouse Alexandrina (The Brown & Hay Families), 76

The Blair Family, 88

The Santas Family, 98

The Skis Family, 118

Part One
Psychic Research Begins

Chapter 1

Mysteries to Solve

"You must write our stories."

As I stepped into the labyrinth, my long dead great-grandmother spoke to me. There was no mistaking the voice in my head as I walked the spiral path. I was attending a creative workshop, set high on a hill above the Mississippi River in western Wisconsin, one hot summer day. Little did I know, I would soon become obsessed with discovering my ancestry.

It began when my Aunt Nan, my mom's younger sister, sent me old family photos. I started to wonder about the generations before me. Who were these people? I was especially interested in the Scottish side of my family. Being half Scottish, I love anything do with Scotland. The beauty of the land, the mystical shape-shifting Kelpie, the tartan plaids of the clans, the castles, and of course the Loch Ness monster, Nessie.

My first mystery involved my great-grandmother who spoke to me telepathically that day in the labyrinth. She was Annie McIntosh Couper. I learned the couple that raised her were not her real parents. Her mother was a servant girl, but who was Annie's father? I felt my ancestors were compelling me to find the truth. With ancestry research I began to uncover a picture of their lives, but at times, I hit roadblocks.

I discovered I was a pretty good detective. The more I looked, the more I found. I was completely captivated. Over the course of two years, I uncovered many family secrets. One being the identity of Annie's true father. Along with a disappearing sea captain descended from pirates and whiskey smugglers. A woman ancestor who died in a poorhouse in Scotland. The mystery of the parentage of my favorite uncle. Another ancestor led me to his land in western Wisconsin and connected me to the 150-year-old spiritualist camp nearby.

It took hours of background work, using all kinds of sources, to dig up the past of each person. My enthusiasm for learning about my great-grandmother's life is a good example. I struggled to find information, and I couldn't let it go. I was at my wits' end when a thought occurred to me. Why not use mediumship and my psychic skills to connect with my ancestors? Maybe they can help. I tried it, and many times it worked. I used this often, but only when all other channels failed to give me the answers I sought.

Because of this unconventional approach, what started out as ancestor research soon turned into much more. The path to uncover their stories rarely followed a straight line. I found many twists, turns and surprises along the way. I also came to know that there are more psychics in my family than me, both living and dead.

As I told my stories and those of my ancestors, I began to question: did all these things really happen to me and my family? Yes, they did. And they are all true, as much as I can know. Memories came flooding back to me, along with newly revealed facts about my living relatives' ghostly experiences. There were many history lessons about the times my ancestors lived in, including social and economic challenges. From 12th century Scotland to the pioneers in America to the present day, the lives of my ancestors came alive in vivid detail.

Within their stories, there is heartbreak and deceit, but also love, success, and magic. Among my ancestors were sea captains and pirates, artists, farmers, settlers, enslavers, psychics, Freemasons, clock makers, factory workers, carpenters, musicians, whiskey barrel makers, inventors and more. But sadly, no kings or queens!

This was also a journey of self-acceptance. The world of the unusual is the psychic world I've always lived in, and it's not easy to share it with others. By combining my stories and research with the active participation of my departed ancestors, a truly fantastic tale has unfolded. But I'm getting ahead. I'll begin with the story of Annie McIntosh Couper, my mother's grandmother and my first use of psychic ancestry.

Annie (McIntosh) Couper

Family Tree for Annie (McIntosh) Couper
My great-grandmother
(Born: Annie Robertson Black)

- Angus McIntosh
- Emeila Chisolm 1st Wife Before Jane
- Jane (Hay) McIntosh 2nd Wife

- Simon McIntosh Son of Angus & Emeila
- James McIntosh Son of Angus & Jane *Not Married to Eliza
- Eliza Black (Elizabeth) Mother of Annie Married to David Duncan

Annie McIntosh Couper ←-------- Raised By ←-------- (Simon McIntosh)

- Frances (Couper) Blair
- Barbara Blair
- Terri Blair

Clan Mackintosh (McIntosh)
The clan motto is "Touch not the cat bot (without) a glove."

Pendant above from celticstudio.com

Chapter 2

The Search for Annie's Real Father

My great-grandmother Annie McIntosh Couper had a ticket to sail on the ill-fated Titanic, but literally missed the boat. She would have traveled from her home in Dundee, Scotland about 500 miles to board the ship in Southampton, England. I don't know exactly what caused her delay that day, but luckily for me, she made it to America a little more than a month later aboard the SS Californian. How brave she was to board an ocean liner heading to New York right after the sinking of the Titanic. Annie was traveling for love. She was to meet up with her future husband, Frederick Couper, who was already living in the United States. He arrived in the U.S. the previous year to escape a life of family responsibility back in Scotland.

Frederick's father was a ship captain, gone at sea for months at a time. As he came of age, he was expected to take over caring for his mother Alexandrina. He was an artist, and this was not the life he envisioned. Annie and Frederick met in a local church in Dundee, Scotland, where she played the organ. They fell in love and Annie was excited to travel to America to join him.

I was only two years old when Annie died and never knew her. I wish I had the chance. Who would have thought that all these years later, I would unravel a mystery surrounding who her real parents were, along with her true age? This discovery was made by combining my psychic skills and nuts-and-bolts ancestry research.

I learned crucial facts about her family that she never knew about in her own lifetime.

Psychic ability is said to run in my family. By psychic, I mean perceptions and experiences that can't be explained by what is considered proper scientific physical reality, in a commonsense way. My mother had psychic talents but was very afraid of them. My Aunt Nan also has psychic experiences, which have been mostly positive, but sometimes very frightening. I haven't always welcomed my own psychic encounters. Later in life, I embraced this side of myself, learned how to be careful and constructive, and now look at it as a gift. Apparently, my great-grandmother Annie had this ability as well. She often had premonitions before events happened, including her own death. She was feeling ill and needed to go to the hospital. On the way out the door, she whispered in her granddaughter's ear, "If I go to the hospital, I won't be coming back." She didn't. Did she have a premonition about the Titanic too? Perhaps in some way she knew something bad was going to happen and that made her late in getting to the ship.

In my ancestry research into my great-grandmother Annie, I used many conventional sources, including Scottish birth records and Ancestry.com. I discovered my great-grandmother Annie McIntosh was born Annie Robertson Black in Elgin, Moray, Scotland, a picturesque town on the River Lossie. One mystery surrounding her was that Annie was raised by Simon and Rebecca McIntosh, whom she believed were her parents, but, as I later discovered, were not. When I found her birth record, I discovered Annie was born the illegitimate daughter of a servant girl named Elizabeth (Eliza) Black in Elgin, Scotland in 1874. Eliza worked as a domestic servant in the household of Jane Hay McIntosh. Eliza's job was very common at the time. Most servants lived in their employer's homes, worked long hours, and didn't make much money. Of course, everyone wants his or her ancestors to be rich, famous, or notorious. Eliza was none of these things. I started digging to find out everything I could about her.

In the late 1800s, the area near Elgin, Moray County, had the third highest incidence of illegitimate children in all of Scotland. Many young girls left the family home at a young age to go to work, some as domestic servants, like Eliza. On Annie's birth record, there was no father listed, just Eliza's name. This was disappointing. I hit a brick wall right away. I didn't know how to start a search for Annie's father. After 1855, it was no longer required to list the child's father's name on the birth record, so the mystery of who Annie's real father was remained.

Annie was raised by Simon and Rebecca McIntosh. Simon McIntosh was 53 years old and already had a wife, Rebecca, and several children when he took her in and raised her as part of his family. At that age he was already close to the life expectancy of most males of the time. Nothing against Simon, but a young girl like Eliza most likely wasn't interested in him.

Intuitively, it didn't feel right that Simon was Annie's father. I felt strongly, there was more to the story. Many of the details I was finding didn't add up. I became determined to find the truth, as though Eliza was pushing me from the other side. So, who was Annie's birth father? I didn't even know where to begin, so I turned to a psychic practice called mediumship.

Using mediumship, I called in Eliza Black. To do this, I went into a meditative state with my eyes closed, asked for protection and for Eliza to "show up." In a few minutes, I noticed her standing in front of me in my mind's eye. In my mediumship sessions I see clear images of the person I'm contacting. She looked a lot like my great-grandmother Annie did when she was young, with long kinky red-gold hair and a slender figure. At first, I thought it was Annie, but she told me telepathically she was Annie's mother, Eliza.

I felt a positive energy coming from her. She looked happy and carefree as she danced and skipped around. I thought I would get right to the point, and asked Eliza who the father of Annie was. She answered, "Jimmy."

Eliza explained she was never in a romantic relationship with Jimmy, but they had a "bit of bawdy fun" which resulted in her becoming pregnant. This statement didn't come from me; I would never talk like that. I knew Eliza was speaking to me, as she would have done in the 1800s. As it turned out, this small bit of information about the name James (Jimmy) is what helped solve the mystery.

Again, using mediumship, I decided to contact my great-grandmother Annie to see if she could provide any further insight. To prove that I was connecting with Annie, I asked her to show me two things that someone in the family could identify. She showed me an image of a tarnished silver spoon, and a circular piece of jewelry with a purple stone in the center of it. This is an example of evidential mediumship, where I ask the deceased person to show me things that can be later verified.

Aunt Nan was following my ancestry progress, so I emailed her to see if any of these objects sounded familiar to her, since she had some of Annie's keepsakes. She immediately emailed back and said a tarnished spoon was part of a display hanging on her wall and, just that morning, the spoon fell off the display. It had been hanging there for ten years and was securely in place, so this was odd. She also sent me a picture of a circular brooch that was my great-grandmother's, with purple stones set in it. It looked like the jewelry Annie showed me. This gave me the chills, but in a good way. Annie was really connecting with me. However, the session ended without any further answers about her parents. Although my great-grandmother didn't give me any new clues, it did make me happy to know she is available in spirit.

The Search for Annie's Real Father

I decided to believe Eliza and use the name James or Jimmy as my starting point in my research into Annie's real father. I wondered why Eliza didn't tell me his exact name. Soon after, I learned that the spirits want me to enjoy the process and telling me would spoil the fun!

In my search, I found a James McIntosh listed on a census record for Simon McIntosh, but he was listed as a boarder, not a son. I then found a birth record for a James McIntosh born in 1854, in Rafford, a village near Elgin. Eliza, Annie's mother, was also from Rafford, born that same year. This was a clue! In a small village like this, they most likely knew each other, and as it turned out, they knew each other pretty well. Finding clues like this is exciting. I felt like a private investigator making progress on a case.

With more digging, I found out that the father of James McIntosh was Angus McIntosh from Rafford. Angus owned and farmed eight acres on the grounds of Blervie Castle. The castle was built in the 1600s and, at one time, was owned by an Alexander Mackintosh. Clan names often have spelling variations of surnames. However, this is the same clan as McIntosh.

Angus McIntosh had two wives. This was not uncommon in those days, since people didn't tend to live that long. With his first wife Emelia, he had a son named Simon (Simon McIntosh). Several years later, Angus was remarried to a woman named Jane Hay. They had a son named James, (James McIntosh). So, Simon and James were brothers, born several years apart with different mothers, but had the same father. This was great information, but it wasn't complete proof that James was indeed Annie's father, although it seemed very likely.

One day, out of the blue, I got an email from Ancestry.com, saying they had a new "hint" for me about Jane Hay McIntosh. I took the bait and clicked on the hint. It was a census record, where Jane listed Annie as her granddaughter. I got really excited about this. To me, this was acknowledgement that her son James was Annie's true father, and she was Annie's grandmother. Annie lived in Jane's household until she was six years old.

Around this time, Simon apparently decided to take Annie in and raise her as his own. As I mentioned, he had several children already, so perhaps another child was not a concern. Annie received the education she wouldn't have had if Eliza raised her. Eliza was illiterate and couldn't sign her own name. She marked an "X" as her signature on Annie's birth record. Also, I believe that Annie didn't know her true age. On the ship manifest from the SS Californian, she claimed she was 33 years old. She was really 38 at the time she sailed. Her obituary listed her as 78 years old when she was actually 85 when she died. I attribute this to Simon taking her in as a young child of six and masking her true identity and age. Legal adoption did not exist in Scotland until 1930; however, Annie's surname became McIntosh.

I felt great. I'd solved a mystery, but more intrigue was to come. Several months later, I was searching for death records to add more detail to the family tree. I found the death record for Eliza Black on www.scottishpeople.uk. The records on this website are excellent and provide great detail. Eliza died when she was 71 years old of "senile decay." Nice way of putting it! Also listed on her death record were her husband's name, a David Duncan, and a witness, her son James Black Duncan (note the name James). Okay, I thought, Eliza eventually got married and had another child. I decided to look up her son's birth record to get an idea of when he was born, since he would be Annie's half-brother. I found the record quickly and looked at it in disbelief. Her son was born the year before Annie in 1873! What? I then scrambled to find the marriage record of Eliza and David. On this record, Eliza was listed as "Betsy" Black and married David Duncan in 1871. This changed the entire story. Eliza was a married woman with a new baby when she became pregnant with Annie by James McIntosh.

If what Eliza told me in our mediumship session is true, her relationship with James (Jimmy) was a voluntary one. I hoped that was true. In any case, according to census records, Eliza continued to live with her husband after giving birth to Annie, but Annie lived in Jane's household until she was six years old and after that in Simon's household. Since Eliza worked for Jane, she could see Annie at her workplace. I wondered how she worked all this out with her husband David. He would have known she was pregnant, but Annie as a child is only listed on Jane Hay McIntosh's census, not the census of David and Eliza.

James McIntosh went on to marry someone else and died young of tuberculosis at the age of 31. He also had a son who would be another half-brother to Annie.

At this point, I thought I would use mediumship and contact Eliza one last time to see if she would confirm the nature of her relationship with James/Jimmy. As I tuned in, she showed up easily and seemed eager to connect. She looked youthful, with her hair up in a loose bun, wearing a long dress. She insisted that it was a consensual relationship with James/Jimmy. She said, "He's different than my husband David, who's very serious. Jimmy was always fun, with a wink and a grin." She showed me a bar of soap and said she worked hard, scrubbing floors even while pregnant. She mentioned that I should check the census records one more time for her and her husband David. I did this and found they had another child, a daughter, named Eliza Duncan. This would mean my great-grandmother Annie had two half-brothers and a half-sister that she never got to know. Annie grew up thinking Simon's children were her siblings. I felt bad for her that she missed out on knowing her true mother and half brothers and sister. Maybe there's a chance she can connect with them in the afterlife.

At the end of this session with Eliza, I thanked her and envisioned her bathed in white light. She started to walk away and turned to blow me a kiss. In that moment, I felt a warmth and true connection to my great-great-grandmother. This was an emotional journey finding out the real parentage of my great-grandmother Annie. I feel like she was learning about all this right along with me.

I still wonder about Eliza's family, especially the women. Were they psychic and passed it on to their daughters? There is much I want to know. But first, I will start with the beginning of my story: my mother, Barbara Blair.

Tarnished spoon on wall display

Annie's thistle pin. The dark stones are purple in color

Chapter 3

My Mother as Ancestor

I felt a jolt when I came across a photo of my mother's gravestone on Ancestry.com. I've never seen this before because I've never visited my mom's grave. Once the wooden box containing her ashes was buried after the funeral, that was it. I never went back. I realize many people visit the graves of their loved ones, but I don't personally believe the souls of the departed hover around their graves waiting for visitors. I think gravesite visits may be more for the comfort of the living than the departed. I loved my mother dearly and I don't think my lack of cemetery visits diminishes this.

My lovely mother lost her battle with depression and took her own life in the summer of 1985. She was forty-six years old. Over the course of my childhood, she tried committing suicide a few times. This time she succeeded with an overdose of sleeping pills.

My mom, Barbara, was the second oldest daughter of Frances Couper Blair. My Aunt Nan who is mentioned often in this story is her younger sister. My mother – my ancestor – has impacted my life in a big way.

Her journey with mental illness started when she was nineteen and was recently married to my father, Jerry. They were high school sweethearts and married when my mom was eighteen. She had three kids by the time she was twenty-five: me, my sister, and my brother. It was not uncommon in the late 1950s and early 1960s to have several children by this age. My father could be charming and witty but was also a jealous and controlling person who made life difficult for his young wife. My mom was not the confined, domestic "Tupperware®" wifey-type of the era. She was a smart, free-spirited and fun-loving person who was thrust into adulthood too fast with the responsibility of a young family.

I don't think being the dutiful mother and housewife so soon into her marriage is what she envisioned. In a short amount of time, my dad became mean and even more controlling, not even allowing her to go to the grocery store alone. My mom became very depressed, and the doctors of the day gave her heavy drugs to try and cure her of her sadness. In the 1950s and early 1960s these drugs were terrible. They were essentially strong tranquilizers that turned her into a zombie with no energy and even produced hallucinations. All she could do was sleep most of the time. To help my dad cope with my mom's situation the doctors thought it was a good idea to give him drugs too. He started taking a drug similar to Valium. Along with all the drugs, they both drank a lot. So it was pretty rough.

My mom was in and out of mental health facilities her entire adult life. Some of which were like horror movie sets with locked doors and bars on the windows, people screaming and crawling on the floor like animals. As part of her treatment, she was given electro-shock treatments to suppress her bad memories. Because of this, as kids, we had to teach her how to count and spell all over again, with the use of flash cards. At one point, my dad threatened to tell the doctors to give her a lobotomy. She lived in mortal terror of this threat.

I spent many years of my childhood visiting her in these places and I knew she didn't belong there. I always felt she was a victim of an emotionally abusive husband and a medieval mental health system, where doctors prescribed drugs and did little else. This may sound harsh, but it is my perspective on the situation. She was never able to break through the haze of drugs to experience life to its fullest, although there were happy moments.

My mom loved Christmas. We didn't have a lot of money, but each year she made the holidays special. On Christmas Eve we all piled into the car and took a drive in the snowy night, to look at lighted decorations around our neighborhood. Once in the car, my mom, aka Santa, would forget her purse in the house and would run in to get it. She didn't really forget her purse; she was inside putting all the gifts under the tree, which would be revealed when we got back from our drive. There were always piles of gifts for all of us. I'm not sure how my parents afforded it, but it made Christmas truly magical.

In between her hospital stays, she had some good times. There were summer picnics at Wisconsin lakes, backyard parties with our aunts, uncles and cousins, neighborhood get-togethers, late night card games with friends, and local baseball games. At these gatherings, Brandy Old-Fashioneds were served to the adults and an endless sugar supply for the kids, plus lots of laughter.

My mom was proud of her Scottish heritage. She loved bagpipes and excelled at making shortbread with the family recipe handed down from her grandmother, Annie McIntosh Couper. Everyone in the family is still sworn to secrecy and cannot reveal the recipe.

My parents did love each other, but their relationship was highly dysfunctional, and they eventually divorced in 1976. After they were divorced, my mom went to live in an apartment in government-subsidized housing and started to build a life of her own. She seemed to be doing much better in those days. When she died, she was packing to move into a new apartment. She was excited to be relocating to a nicer neighborhood. It was a surprise that she ended her life when she did.

I always felt a close bond with my mom, even though growing up, I didn't spend very much time with her. We had social workers that took care of us when she was in the hospital, along with neighbor families that sort of adopted us and helped take care of us. My mom didn't drive, so when I was older, I would sometimes take her for long drives in the country, which she loved. I became more of a friend to her and less like a daughter. She confided in me about her relationships and how she was treated over the years. Even though there are three children in our family, each person's relationship with our parents was different.

Shortly after she died, she came to me in a dream and told me she was fine, but she didn't like the house they had her living in. A few years later, she came to me in a dream again. This time she was getting on a bus and told me she was moving to a better place. The dreams were not like usual dreams, they were very vivid, and I felt she was actually there talking to me, and I've never forgotten them.

When I started with my mediumship training, I did a session where I asked the spirit of my mom to connect with me. She showed up dressed in a great outfit. She was wearing a pencil skirt with a beautifully tailored matching jacket, like Grace Kelly wore in the movie *Rear Window*. She looked beautiful! She told me she was happy and that she was now starting over and re-living her life, starting in the 1950s. In the spirit world, she intended to recreate her life experience in a positive and happy way, so she could change the negative pattern. Of course, there is no way to prove something like this, but it did make me feel like she was working towards positive change on the other side.

In readings I've had with other mediums, my mom often comes through with messages for me. Most recently, she gave me encouragement on my ancestry work and wants me to keep going with the research. She is aware of what I'm working on and is cheering me on.

Having a psychic connection with a loved one can be very healing. For me it's a way to communicate with my mom and to know that she's free of suffering and lives on in spirit. I may not visit my mother's grave, but I honor her in many ways by sending her love, good thoughts, and empathy.

Through mediumship and research, I've found many more women ancestors. Like my mother, they've struggled with many things. Eliza had an illegitimate child; she didn't reveal who the father was. She watched Annie be raised by another family. As you'll learn in the coming chapters about the Blairs and Coupers, my ancestor Mary Blair lost six of her thirteen children. The Couper women were married to sea captains, so they were left alone for years at a time to raise their families. In the Blair family, some were pioneers in the early days of America, starting a new life without knowing what the future would hold. Many crossed the ocean to settle in America.

All these women, including my mother, are part of my tribe. I feel their presence with me, as I get to know their stories. Energetically on some level, I think they know I'm looking for them and that they are not forgotten.

Author's parents in 1955. Barbara was 17 years old at the time.

Psychic Ancestry

Barbara Blair gravestone

Chapter 4
A Psychic Journey

Mediumship has always intrigued me, but I was a little bit afraid. My understanding of mediumship was that it's a process where I or a third party (another medium) attempts to contact a deceased person, to ask them specific questions or to receive messages from them. I thought if I delved into learning mediumship, unintended things would start to happen. Maybe spirits would materialize in front of me or haunt my house. In the fall of 2021, I decided to put aside my fears about trying to contact the dead and take a class to see what I could learn. And to see if I could actually do it.

I began learning mediumship about the same time I was immersed in researching my family's history. I was interested in adding a new skill to my many years of practicing directed meditation and psychic development. It was a way to help others connect with departed loved ones to bring closure and comfort. Initially, I didn't think about using spirit communication to connect with my ancestors. That came later, as I hit stumbling blocks in my research, and realized I could try to reach out directly to my ancestors for answers.

My journey with the spirit world started when I was very young. This came in the form of hauntings, ghostly apparitions, and other paranormal activity. Later, I experienced premonitions, psychic visions and now communication with spirits and guides.

Psychic Ancestry

When I was five years old, my family lived across the street from an old cemetery. Our house was the lower portion of a duplex, where I shared a bedroom with my sister. She was a deep sleeper and was oblivious to the world around her at night. I had a much different experience. Many nights, I was awakened by a pulsing energy that felt like it was pressing on me and made me feel sick. It's hard to explain what this felt like. The best way to describe it is that I felt pressure on my body that would come and go in waves, along with a nauseous feeling. It was terrible and I felt like I had no control over it and couldn't stop it. I would finally fall back asleep, but it was very disturbing, and I would purposely try to stay awake so the feeling wouldn't come, but it usually did. I never told my parents or anyone about it. My parents were young at the time, almost like kids having kids. They were emotionally distant, involved in their own drama with each other, so I didn't feel I could tell them about this. I also didn't think I could really explain what was happening to me in a way they would understand, so I kept it to myself. I didn't want to scare my sister either, so I never mentioned anything to her.

Decades later, long after I had moved away, I would find out something important from a friend, which really helped put this whole ordeal into perspective. During the 1990s he worked on a street repair project in the area, in front of our old duplex. The project was to dig up and widen the road in front of the house. As they started removing earth, they uncovered three layers of bones buried beneath the street. The bones were determined to be Native American children's bones, most likely from the Potawatomi tribe that had lived in the area, although this has not been confirmed. It was assumed they all died of a disease, perhaps smallpox, and were buried in a mass grave. According to this friend, the bones were removed and re-buried elsewhere. I believe it was the spirits of these children who haunted me each night. Perhaps these children died too young, and resented a kid like me. I was alive and living out my childhood and they couldn't.

When I found this out, I had an overwhelming sense of relief. I had some sort of answer for the nighttime episodes. It made complete sense to me that the untimely deaths of infants and children buried in the cemetery along with the bodies beneath the street all added up to unsettled spirits. I believe this was the beginning of my psychic awareness, which I went on to cultivate into positive experiences in the years ahead.

My interest in all things psychic really ramped up when I was in my early 20s. I spent many hours learning to meditate and to use my psychic skills, such as clairvoyance. Luckily, I've had some great teachers along the way. I joined a group in Milwaukee that met once a week. At class, we sat in colorful beanbag chairs, and our instructor led us in guided meditations and other activities, such as doing psychic readings for each other. We did other exercises like psychometry to open up and learn to trust our intuition. Psychometry is a practice where one holds an object that belongs to another person and receives psychic impressions from it. For instance, a woman handed me a key, and as I held it, I envisioned a small space with shelves filled with blue glass bottles. The woman then verified the key was to her very small house and she owned a collection of blue glass vases.

This class became like therapy for me, as it gave me a sense of belonging. It was a group of positive people learning to use their own abilities. I had success, which really helped boost my confidence. I was able to give people psychic readings that were accurate and often helped them to gain clarity on a situation. It's important to note that all people have these abilities if they choose to learn how to use them. I often wonder, why wouldn't everyone be interested in learning about how to use his or her own psychic skills? Exploring this has added more dimensions to my life.

I also taught myself how to read Tarot cards. I studied some books on the subject, and then received my first Tarot deck as a gift. I took my time and learned what each card meant. Tarot cards are a great tool for using intuition and receiving psychic messages. I've read the cards for friends and for myself ever since getting my first deck. I had a group of friends who lived in my apartment complex, who frequently asked me to read their cards; mostly they wanted information about their love lives. They requested this almost daily! We would meet after dinner, and I would answer their questions, using the cards. There were various love triangles going on in the group, so it got tricky at times.

Throughout these years, I often traveled to Virginia Beach, Virginia, to study at the Edgar Cayce Institute, The Association for Research and Enlightenment (A.R.E.), and moved there for one year when I was 28 years old. Edgar Cayce (1877-1945) was a famous American clairvoyant. I first learned about him by reading *There is a River,* by Thomas Sugrue. It's the story of Cayce and how he became known as "The Sleeping Prophet." The library at the A.R.E. has 14,000 of Cayce's psychic readings that form the core of his work, and houses one of the largest collections of metaphysical books in the world with 80,000 volumes. I spent many days at the A.R.E researching the readings, parapsychology, and holistic health. Over the years, I attended classes led by world-renowned channelers, energy healers, mediums, psychic practitioners, and archeologists who gave the latest updates about ancient mysteries.

My favorite uncle, George, my dad's brother, was the person who first got me interested in Edgar Cayce. George was an engineer by trade and was gifted with a curious mind about spiritual metaphysics. He was also a bit of a mad scientist. He made holograms in his basement on his pool table with lasers and mirrors long before holography became a common technology. Once each summer over a ten-year time span, I traveled with George and my dad Jerry to the white sand beaches of Virginia to study at the A.R.E. During our long car rides from Wisconsin to the beach, George and I would discuss, debate, and try to figure out what the hell Stephen Hawking was taking about.

I always looked forward to this yearly trip. My flexible work schedule made it possible to take a few weeks off. After we arrived in Virginia Beach, we would settle into a 60s-style oceanside motel called The Marshalls. The motel had seen better days, but it sat right on the beach and had breathtaking views. The first time we stayed there, I cried when I saw the room. It was furnished with old, outdated furniture and smelled moldy. The curtains and bedspread looked to be the originals from 1963, with sea foam green and royal blue flower prints. And of course, shag carpeting on the floors. However, I soon forgot about the crusty motel room, as I began meeting many fascinating people at the seminars. Later, there would be regulars who showed up every year.

They were a diverse group of holistic practitioners, teachers, businessmen and women, therapists, nurses, and people from all over the world who came to learn and to meet like-minded people. After the daytime classes, several of us would gather at The Marshalls for a drink after dinner to talk about what we learned. There was an oceanside community room where everyone would meet. It was furnished with old rattan furniture and a bar, but no bartender. If you wanted a drink, you could buy a plastic cup full of wine from the front desk clerk for five dollars. She kept a small fridge under the reception desk stocked with wine bottles.

There were parties going on almost every night at someone's house or at The Marshalls. For a spiritual group, I was amazed at the amount of romantic hook-ups and partying. We spent so much time during the day in classes, meditating and self-reflecting, that at night everyone got a little wild. It must have been the ocean air!

George and my dad were interested in the Cayce readings for their holistic health recommendations and attended health-related lectures and seminars. And they had another important reason to be there. George and my dad, both divorcés, were dedicated to hitting on the lovely women who came to the seminars, often fighting over the same one for the entire trip. If my dad sat down next to a woman he was interested in, George would show up and sit down on the other side of her and try and get her attention. It was a constant competition. Neither George nor Jerry fared well in their pursuits, but it was fun to watch.

I learned so much over the years at the A.R.E. and made lasting friendships. I'm still a member and continue to take their online classes and use the holistic remedies I learned so much about. It still thrives today, in the original research institute.

In my forties, I studied extensively with the late Richard Sutphen, a hypnotist and psychic development seminar leader and author of many metaphysical books. I first met Richard on a trip with some girlfriends to beautiful Sedona, Arizona. That weekend was spent meeting new people and doing all kinds of psychic exercises. Richard knew where the energy vortexes were in Sedona and took the class on hiking trips to find them. The energy vortexes are believed to be special spots on the earth where energy is either entering or projecting out of the earth's plane. There are several other vortex sites throughout the world such as the Great Pyramid in Egypt and Machu Picchu in Peru.

One of the vortexes in Sedona is on Airport Mesa. This is where I first experienced the vortex energy. After climbing up to a certain spot on the mesa, I sat and waited skeptically to see if anything would happen. Sitting quietly, I noticed what looked like a wavy grid pattern in the air coming up out of the ground. I thought I was seeing things, but it was there and didn't disappear after several minutes of watching it. It was amazing. I didn't feel anything special but could definitely see it. The pattern stayed in place but was not static; it had an undulating motion to it. Others could not see the energy the way that I perceived it, and some had their own experience of this phenomenon. I also noticed it in other hiking spots in Sedona. From then on, every time I visit Sedona, I make a point to visit the same spot to look for this energy, and usually I experience it again. Richard Sutphen died in September of 2020. I feel honored to have known him.

Later, I studied with Richard's ex-wife, Tara Sutphen, also in Arizona. Tara is a gifted mystic, astrologer and psychic. Tara and Richard were divorced when I started taking classes from her. She has a different teaching style than Richard, so I learned different techniques to do psychic readings for people. It's always so fun when I get something right when giving a reading. It's certainly not 100 percent correct, but I feel it's helpful.

However, with all the training I had over the years on various subjects, mediumship was not something I studied with any of my teachers. As I delved into my ancestry work, there were mysteries that traditional research did not solve for me. I was excited to try a new approach. Even if a person has psychic abilities, it doesn't mean they can also be a medium. It's not an automatic talent, it takes practice, and results are not guaranteed.

To begin learning mediumship, I joined a class with an experienced teacher. I began with anticipation, but again with some skepticism, since I'd never tried this before. One of the first exercises the teacher gave me was to pick a famous person and see if I could contact him or her. The instructions were to ask the person three things I didn't know about him or her that could later be verified, using evidential mediumship.

For this exercise, I decided to contact Hedy Lamarr. A few years back, I'd read a book about Hollywood stars and Hedy was mentioned. She was the only daughter of a wealthy family in Vienna and would become a star during Hollywood's golden age. In Austria, she was married to a rich, much older man who was very controlling. One day, she dressed as her maid and escaped her house and stifling marriage. She eventually ended up in Hollywood. I was drawn to Hedy because of her beauty, intelligence, and courage. It was great that she found a way to escape her restrictive husband. In the U.S. she became an inventor as well as a talented actress. At the height of her film career in and the middle World War II, she and a musician and fellow inventor named George Antheil invented the basis for all modern wireless communications called signal hopping. In my own life, and on a much smaller scale, I'm co-inventor of a line of lighted makeup mirrors. And I love a bit of glamour. I felt a kinship.

When I was ready to contact Hedy in a session, I sat quietly in meditation and imagined myself surrounded by white protective light. The type of meditation I do uses imagery and visualization techniques, so the image of Hedy came into my mind and I asked her to join me.

We started walking together into a room that looked like a movie star's dressing room. In the room was a makeup table with a big lighted mirror. A shoulder mink stole was draped over a plush chair. As we stood in the room together, I felt she was ready to communicate. I needed something I didn't know about her that could be later verified, so I asked her how tall she was in her adult life. She replied telepathically, "5 feet, 7 inches." She also mentioned that being a movie star was not as glamorous as it looks. The pancake makeup was awful! She said that Alfred Hitchcock was notorious for pinching women and so she steered clear of him. After this brief exchange, I ended the session, thanked her, and visualized her walking away in a bright white light. Then I ran straight to my computer and looked up her height, which was confirmed to be 5 feet, 7 inches. I also found a picture on the internet of her wearing the same mink stole draped across her shoulders, and several sources that noted the bad behavior of old Alfred. I didn't know any of these things before I did the exercise. This was amazing! When I started the session, I wasn't sure what to expect and was happy to get a good result. It didn't feel scary or out of control. This was my very first exercise using mediumship and I was astounded that it was that easy to contact a spirit.

For another exercise, I tried to connect with my good friend Mary's Uncle Oscar, who died long before I knew Mary. Oscar Zerk was an interesting person, also Austrian-born, and a world-famous inventor. He patented over 300 inventions including leg-slimming hosiery. You've got to love that! One of his most important inventions was a grease fitting known as "The Zerk Fitting", which is still in use today.

Oscar owned a three-story mansion in Kenosha, Wisconsin, called "Dunmovin." The house stood on thirty-two acres of land with beautiful landscaping and peony gardens. He renovated the house to be art deco style and it was full of unique and original artwork he acquired on his travels around the world. Oscar was very social and hosted grand dinner parties at his home. One report has it that if guests showed up 15 minutes late, Oscar met them at the door in a dressing gown. He informed them of their tardiness and told them he was about to retire, closed the door and went upstairs.

Oscar passed away in 1968 and was survived by his wife Dorothy. Dorothy, Mary's aunt, was Oscar's fourth wife. Oscar and Dorothy had a happy marriage, and when Dorothy passed away many years later, Mary asked me to help her clean out the mansion. We spent weekends over a year's time working on this project. The house had a personality of its own. Whenever I was there, I could feel the presence of someone, maybe the spirit of Oscar, watching us move about the house.

I don't really know why I chose to contact Oscar, except that I thought he was an interesting person in life and thought it would be fun to finally meet him in spirit.

In the mediumship session, Oscar appeared in my mind's eye, impeccably dressed in a suit and classy shoes with his hair perfectly groomed. He looked just like pictures I'd seen of him when he was younger. I asked him for any messages he would like to give to Mary that would prove I was actually contacting him. He said he remembered her as a child with big brown eyes, playing the piano in his dining room. He also said, "Show her this crystal dome." The dome was clear glass and fit in the palm of his hand. I couldn't exactly show Mary what I saw in my mind, but I described the look of the crystal to her. Mary confirmed that, at that time, the piano was in the dining room of his home when she played it, although it was later moved to the living room where I saw it. I wouldn't have known it was ever in the dining room. Oscar did own a large crystal collection that was sold after he died. I didn't remember this collection from cleaning out the house, since a lot of the valuables were sold at auction before we started cleaning. Mary also confirmed he was always dressed elegantly in beautifully tailored suits.

I was so excited over these experiences with mediumship. I could connect with the dead, and these particular people were interested in talking with me. But I also learned that it doesn't always work. Perhaps it takes significant effort on their part as well as mine. It may be that spirits need to believe they can connect by transcending time and space. As I would find out later, not all the ancestors I tried to contact would come through, so maybe their own belief systems held them back from being able to make contact. Or maybe they're just not interested. Reincarnation could be a factor too. The person may have moved on to their next life and isn't available to connect as the spirit of the historical person.

There's still so much we don't know about what happens in the afterlife, which makes it a fascinating subject to explore.

So now you know my mother's story, and mine, and how I came to do the hard work of ancestry research. And to turn to my psychic skills when I hit a roadblock. I realized later, it was only my hours of conventional research that allowed me to accept the things I learned in the psychic sessions, because I could verify what I learned there and match it with conventional sources. A foot in both places. Well, most of the time.

Now, on to Eliza's family and the other Scottish clans. There are more riddles to solve.

Author's dad [Jerry] with Uncle George at the A.R.E. in Virginia Beach, 1980s. Edgar Cayce's Institute of Research and Enlightenment

Part Two
The Clans
(McIntosh, Couper, Blair, Mathieson)

Photo credit: Dreamstime.com

Family Tree for Eliza Black's Family
(The Highland Women)
Note: This is not a complete family tree

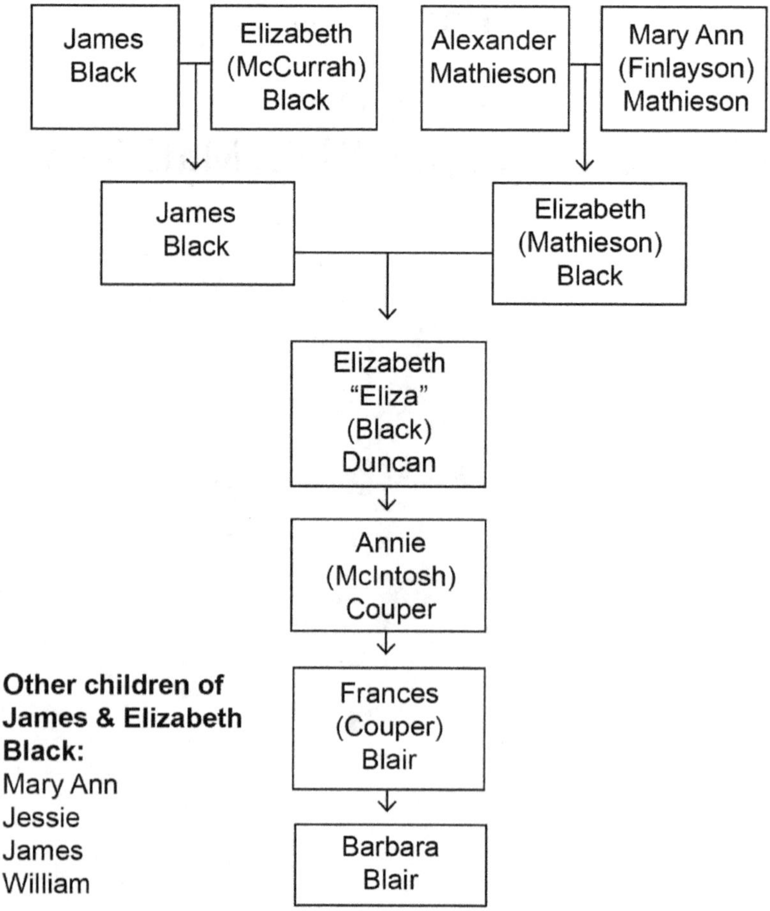

- James Black + Elizabeth (McCurrah) Black → James Black
- Alexander Mathieson + Mary Ann (Finlayson) Mathieson → Elizabeth (Mathieson) Black
- James Black + Elizabeth (Mathieson) Black → Elizabeth "Eliza" (Black) Duncan
- Elizabeth "Eliza" (Black) Duncan → Annie (McIntosh) Couper
- Annie (McIntosh) Couper → Frances (Couper) Blair
- Frances (Couper) Blair → Barbara Blair

Other children of James & Elizabeth Black:
Mary Ann
Jessie
James
William

Chapter 5
The Highland Women

At times in my life, it helps me to have a psychic reading. I was feeling stuck in my ancestor research and thought some insight might help. With the discovery that my great-grandmother Annie was born illegitimate to Eliza Black, I wanted to know more about Eliza's roots and where she came from. Eliza's family was from a rural area in the Scottish Highlands, and I sensed there was a strong link between her family lineage and my psychic abilities.

I asked a friend who does psychic work to do a reading for me. She and I briefly discussed my work in learning about my ancestors. Then she started the reading. She saw three women in her mind's eye. They were on my mom's side of the family. They shared with her that they all were psychic, and the oldest of the three could see events in her mind in great detail before they happened.

The next morning, as I was getting ready for the day, I felt the urge to grab one of my tarot decks and pull a card. The card was the three of cups. It shows three women dancing happily around a maypole. The card represents true friendship and kinship. I intuited that the three women in the reading, and symbolized on the tarot card, are my 2nd great grandmother Eliza, her mother Elizabeth, and her grandmother Mary Ann.

I realize there is no way to find out if these women were psychic, but what if they were? Perhaps it makes sense that this gift would be passed down the family line. Their lives would have been shaped by their abilities and how to work with them, most likely in secret. I realized the only way I could confirm this is through spirit communication. I was excited to start connecting with them in this way. But first, I wanted to get a feel for what their lives were like in the Scottish Highlands in the years they lived there.

The Mathiesons, Blacks and Finlaysons are all Highland clans. Mary Ann (Finlayson) Mathieson was probably born around 1805. Her daughter Elizabeth lived from 1834 to 1928, and her daughter Eliza lived from 1854-1923. They lived in and around the small village of Rafford in Moray County (Morayshire). At one time, the area was a royal burgh, of which there were many in Scotland. Royal burghs were created by the Scottish crown beginning in the 13th century and each was granted a royal charter to have some say in running its local affairs. Often, there were castles in the burghs where visiting royalty would set up court for a season, to mix and celebrate with the local notables, and to keep an eye on things.

Rafford is a farming community. The soil is fertile and has many forests of oak and Scottish firs. The Findhorn River bounds the village. The river is known as one of the fastest and most dangerous of any in Scotland. The town has a large handsome church (Church of Scotland, called the Established Church) in the town center, built in 1826. And there are other churches, including the Free Church of Scotland, which was created in 1843 when it broke from the Established Church. The Free Church opposed the current system of the time that allowed rich landowners to select the local ministers. That did not sit well with most people. The two churches eventually came together around 1900. There were lots of arguments about this at the time according to the local papers. Maybe my ancestors belonged to one of the churches. This would have been a place where they could socialize and be accepted but would not have to reveal what went on in their inner worlds.

The village had four schools and one public-house or inn, a

place for the townsfolk to have a drink. There were several attempts to open more public-houses, but a church minister rejected the idea. Oh well, there were ways to work around this. Rafford was also known for its smugglers. Whiskey, rum, and brandy would be hidden in the hills in the area. Although the authorities looked the other way. Maybe another inn wasn't necessary.

I have never lived in a small town, but I imagine everyone knew about each other to some degree. The town had its share of local characters. This excerpt from a newspaper article was written about a Rafford "wanderer."[1]

> *Wandering Characters-Sandy-No-More*
> *Sandy-No-More was a quiet creature-scarcely ever been angry. He wore a kilt, an article of dress that seemed to be made out of at least thirty remnants of cloth darned firmly together. Summer and winter, straw ropes twisted firmly around his legs served as stockings. On his back was a large sack with his belongings. His appearance on the road resembled a stack of hay in motion. Sandy was a terror to no one. He was a wanderer for nearly thirty years.*

The area had two castles called Burgie and Blervie, twins. They were built near each other and were laid out in the same configuration. Both castles date to around 1600, although Blervie Castle had a fireplace with the year 1398 inscribed on it, so it may have been built on an earlier site. According to a tax roll, James Black, Elizabeth's husband, and Eliza's father, worked as a farm steward or laborer on land surrounding a mansion on the Blervie Castle estate. In these years, the castle was in ruins, but there were other homes on the land. It was common for castles and manor houses to lease their land to people willing to live on it and tend the gardens or

---

[1] *Forres, Elgin and Nairn Gazette*, (1877)

farm the land. A family could lease a dwelling house and could also rent an ox or a cow. As tenant farmers or crofters, they were paid for their produce, hay, grain, and for wood from felled trees, which was used for building and sometimes for burning.

Several times a year, fairs were held where potential tenant farmers and their families were put on display for landowners. The landowners could select a man, woman, or family to work on their land. If hired, the stay at the farm could be brief, not even a year's time. My ancestors would have lived a nomadic life if that was the case for them. In looking through tax rolls and some census records, I was able to determine that the family of James Black did move several times. However, they stayed in the same general area around the village of Rafford.

I think it would be hard to put your family up for hire and move every couple of years. The fairs were almost like auctions where the family members would stand up in front of potential landowners and describe their skills. Moving often could be disruptive, even if moving just a few miles. My ancestors wouldn't have been able to truly call a place home for any length of time. When I was growing up, we moved a few times as kids and it was hard to start over with friendships and schools, plus adjust to a new living space.

An interesting note is that the McIntosh family also lived on Blervie Hill, the part of the Blervie estate where the tenants lived. James McIntosh was the father of Annie (daughter of Eliza). The entire Blervie estate, originally owned by the Dunbar family, a famous land-owning clan in Moray, was purchased by Alexander McIntosh in 1724. With the purchase, McIntosh became Laird of Blairie (Blervie). There is a good chance my ancestor, Angus McIntosh, father of James McIntosh, is a descendant of this man. Angus was born in Rafford and lived and worked on Blervie Hill. He is listed as illegitimate on his death record. His mother was a servant girl, and his father is simply listed as "McIntosh", with no first name. Since Eliza Black and James McIntosh's families both lived and worked here, this must be how they met.

Rafford is a historic and mystical place. The known human history dates at least as far back as the time of the Druids, as well as to the ancient Vikings, Romans, Picts, Celts, and Gaels. Near Blervie Castle are four large standing stones forming a square. They're called the Temple Stones and are evidently the remains of a Druid temple. This is one of several temple ruins in the area. The ancient places of worship were often in shady groves under tall trees or in high places. Rafford had both. The Druids had been instructors in the mysteries of religion, philosophy, and morality. They also shared their wisdom of healing, herbalism, storytelling, and astrology. There were female druids or priestesses who performed some of the rituals and ceremonies. At one time, Druids were held in great regard, although in later centuries, they were influenced by the Romans and were led into superstition and human sacrifice. I've always been fascinated by the Druids and wonder what positive traits of theirs were passed down the generations.

Nearby in the town of Forres stands an obelisk called Sueno's Stone. It reaches 23 feet above the ground and is said to be 12 feet underground. The stone dates to between AD600 and AD1000. It's the largest surviving Pictish style stone in Scotland. The Picts were known as the painted people and were fierce warriors. The stone is decorated with a Celtic cross and once contained figures of men, beasts, and human heads, but is now deteriorated. It appears to depict a battle scene or victory of some sort. It's possible that the lineage of families in the area may go back to the ancient Celts, but I am not sure how to confirm this. The largest group of known descendants of the Celts today are in Ireland, followed by Scotland, Wales and Cornwall.

In Scotland, ancestor records are well preserved. But as I moved up the family tree, records for Elizabeth Mathieson Black and Mary Ann Finlayson Mathieson were proving difficult to find. Historical information about the women in a family can be minimal. Often in ancestry work, the men carry the official written history. That's why oral traditions and storytelling in a family and in a culture are so important.

One day, I felt the women around me. They wanted to communicate. I sat down with a notebook and listened telepathically to their words. It was three women, but the information came as one voice:

We are Mary Ann, Lizze and Eliza. Work on the farms was hard, but we all had our inner lives. And our children. Psychic gifts, we were born with. It goes way back in time when our distant ancestors cultivated this. There was no fear like the fear we felt. We knew the lives of others at a glance. It wasn't hard to see. The witch trials were not that far behind us, so it was in our thoughts. We were on guard. We kept our gifts to ourselves. Elizabeth Mathieson Black could see spirits. They seemed to always be in the room, talking to her. Old soldiers and even their animals. We hushed her so she knew not to speak of it with strangers. We kept this in the family. We could see if a woman would have a difficult birth or if a child would die. We made charms for luck and hoped it would not happen. This is not an easy gift to have.

I could sense their fear of persecution at revealing their true natures. It is something that I struggle with today, even though being burned at the stake is no longer a concern. In Rafford's history in the 1600s and 1700s, there is frequent references to witchcraft, curses, healing practices, divination, and exorcism. Even though by the middle part of the 19th century, after a hundred years or more passed since the witch hunts in Scotland, the atmosphere of superstition prevailed in the countryside of Moray County.

I recently came across the University of Edinburgh's map of witches in Scotland, a database created in 2003 from "The Survey of Scottish Witchcraft." It shows the names of accused witches and gives trial details for several men and women in specific towns. Some of the trial notes include the following categories a witch could include in their confession, almost like a checklist: Demonic pacts, communing with non-natural beings, witches' meetings and meeting places, musical instruments, folk culture, elf and fairy elements, shape changing, ritual objects, diseases or illness, damage to property and weather modification.

Throughout history, the people accused of being witches, both men and women, were often people who worked for free and helped people with their knowledge of natural healing methods. If a person lived at the fringes of society at any capacity or if they were poor, they could be at risk of being included as a target during the witch trials. A marking or birthmark on a body could be enough of a reason to be suspicious of someone. Or sometimes a person was simply disliked and was singled out as a witch.

One story of an accused witch says that she was tortured until she admitted she could shape-shift into a dog. Now that would be a feat. The town of Elgin, which is near Rafford, had 23 trials from 1500 to the 1700s, which was significant. Some estimates put the number of witches tried in Scotland at more than 4,000 prior to the 18th century. By 1736, the Witchcraft Act was thrown out, but it didn't erase the stigma associated with certain kinds of unusual behavior. Today, there are many people who identify as witches and magic practitioners.

I sat down one afternoon to see if I could contact the three women again, using mediumship. I saw one of the women in my mind's eye. She identified herself as Mary Ann, the oldest of the three. She was seated in a chair. In her lap was a handheld harp. The wood of the instrument was worn and faded. She told me she would sing songs that had a spell woven into the lyrics. Only the women knew this, but it was a way to work magic. She also showed me a bag of hand carved rune stones that she used for divination. They were polished stones, different colors with a symbol carved on each. For many years, I have used rune stones to give readings for my friends.

Runes are marked with a series of symbols and shapes, each with its own meaning interpreted by the reader. I also like spells. They are a good way to focus energy. A spell can be used like a positive affirmation. I feel the spells that Mary Ann sang were to create a good outcome of a certain situation. Maybe she sang a spell for a good crop or to bring the family luck or healing from an illness.

Perhaps the women in the family were herbalists. Botanical medicine is an old tradition in Scotland, along with the medicinal use of whiskey. Living close to the land as they did, they would know the native plants and their uses. Not everyone in a given area was an herbalist, but Elizabeth, Eliza's mother, lived to be 94 years old, and her grandmother Mary Ann lived to be 93. They certainly had something going for them. That seems amazing to me given the rustic environment they lived in. It's also likely that they ate fresh food all the time since they lived in an area near the famous garden town of Findhorn.

When I was young, I became fascinated by the story of Findhorn when I saw a photo of a gigantic strawberry. At the time, I had no idea it was in Scotland. In the 1960s, three people founded the Findhorn community. Findhorn is on the coast near Rafford and has barren sandy soil. One of the three founders needed to feed her family on a tight budget, so she decided to use meditation to contact the higher intelligence of plants. "Intelligence" meant the angels and devas (nature spirits) of the area. They gave her instructions on how to make the most of her garden in the sandy soil. She followed the guidance and grew huge plants, herbs, and flowers, and famously 40-pound cabbages! Rafford is seven miles from Findhorn.

I found an article about medical folklore in the area.[2] There were many customs and traditions of the people. There was a varied list of means and modes of cure, many of great antiquity. One cure for whooping cough was to live in a house where the husband and wife both had the same birth surname. Perhaps a change in air was the more important reason to move in with them. To fix a sprain, one could tie a red piece of string around the leg or ankle. Or bury a piece of meat to get rid of warts or immerse silver in water and drink it to banish evil. Many herbal mixes were used as well. This article was written at the same time as the Gilded Age in America and the creation of the modern industrial economy. In contrast, the Highlands were worlds apart.

The life of the Highland women was one of physically demanding farm work, along with taking care of their families, living off the land, and developing their own talents. There was also a mystique to this area. The term "second sight" originated in the Highlands with the Gaels, who had many words referring to it, such as seer. In Scotland, second sight or the gift of premonition, is believed to run in families. Because people in this area lived close to nature, they were in tune with the earth and its subtle energies. Maybe there were many women like my ancestors in rural Scotland. And if so, they may have hidden their abilities unless asked to use them. It may not have been only women, but interestingly in most psychic development classes I attend today, the participants are nearly all women.

The connection with my three female ancestors has triggered memories of times in my life when I was afraid to admit my psychic side. Years ago, people would ask me to tell them my ghost stories.

---

[2] *Northern Notes and Queries of the Scottish Highlands,* (1892)

Psychic Ancestry

Several times, I enthusiastically recounted interesting ghost stories to friends and colleagues. Most of these people never spoke to me again. Many times, at a therapist's office, I would reveal I had psychic experiences. I would get a sideways look as the therapist leaned over and reached for the prescription pad. With the writing of my stories, I'm revealing much about my unconventional life. But I want to do this because it's an important and exciting part of who I am.

To me, the unseen world is such a natural part of our human existence. Why be afraid of it? Many are conditioned not to rely on intuition. It's okay to have a purely logical view of the universe, but there is so much more to be discovered.

Even though this is speculation, I choose to believe that Eliza and the women that came before her had very strong psychic abilities that were passed down the family tree, to me, my mother, my aunt, and perhaps some others. It's very possible that some of my Scottish ancestors were clairvoyant and could see the future. My only proof is my inner voice that tells me this is so.

Tarot card representing the 3 of Cups. Universal Celtic Tarot, Author: Floreana Nativo, Illustrations by Christina Scagliotti

Example of a Scottish farm servant with cow, 1866.
National Records of Scotland (NRS).

Ruins of Blervie Castle in Rafford, Morayshire,
Scotland. Photo credit: Dreamstime.com

Frederick Couper

Family Tree for Frederick Couper
My great-grandfather, married to Annie (McIntosh) Couper
Note: Not all of the Couper children are included here.

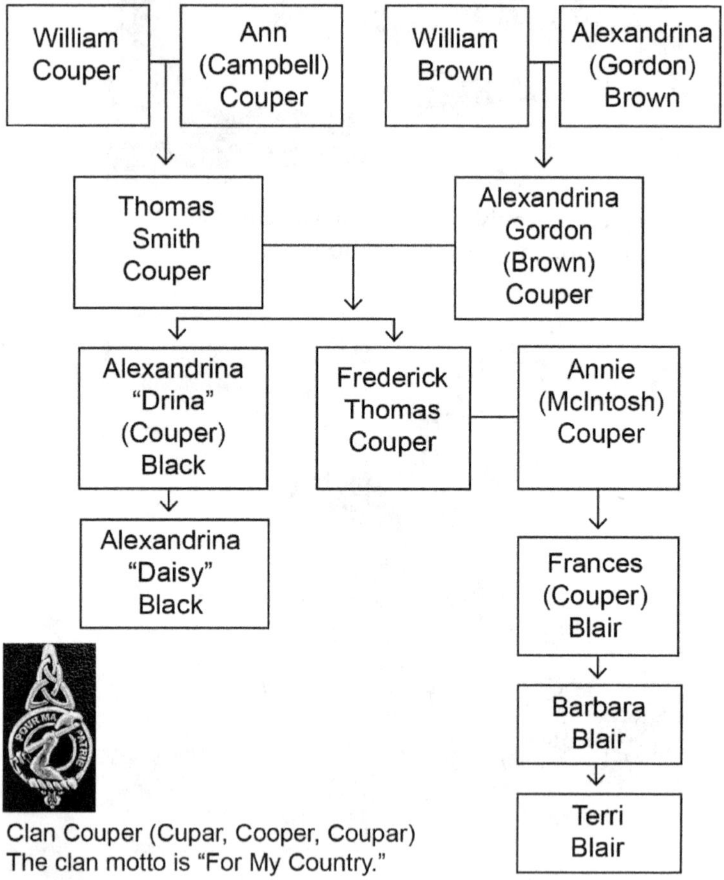

```
William Couper — Ann (Campbell) Couper        William Brown — Alexandrina (Gordon) Brown
                │                                            │
           Thomas Smith Couper ─────────────── Alexandrina Gordon (Brown) Couper
                                    │
        ┌───────────────────────────┼───────────────────────┐
   Alexandrina                 Frederick                Annie
   "Drina"                     Thomas      ─────       (McIntosh)
   (Couper) Black              Couper                  Couper
        │                                                  │
   Alexandrina                                         Frances
   "Daisy"                                             (Couper) Blair
   Black                                                  │
                                                      Barbara Blair
                                                          │
                                                      Terri Blair
```

Clan Couper (Cupar, Cooper, Coupar)
The clan motto is "For My Country."
The name was occupational for a cooper, which is a maker of barrels.

Pendant above from celticstudio.com

Chapter 6

A Mysterious Photo Appears

It's known that my ancestors from the Couper family line were notorious sea pirates and smugglers. In a way, I'm thrilled about this. I have a romantic notion that they were like Johnny Depp as Captain Jack Sparrow in the movie *Pirates of the Caribbean*, although I'm sure the real pirates looked pretty bad and smelled even worse. They were no doubt involved in all kinds of wickedness. Maybe my ancestor pirates turned to this lifestyle out of desperation. I really hope so. Pirates could be robbers or murderers. Some were known to plunder other ships and raid coastal towns. If there's any good news in this, it's that they were experienced sailors. I don't have details about what type of pirates the Coupers were, but I'm hoping they were of the thieving variety and nothing worse.

My great-grandmother Annie McIntosh's husband Frederick Couper was the descendent of these pirates. The lineage of the Coupers traces back to the 12th century. Originally part of the Gordon Clan, they were seafarers who lived around the river Tweed in Southeast Scotland, in an area bordering England and Scotland that served as a buffer between the two kingdoms, with the Cheviot Hills as a backdrop. It was a lawless place, ruled by neither England nor Scotland. Raiders or "Reivers" were a constant terror to anyone who lived there. Reivers were raiding families that took land and property as they wanted. This was not a swashbuckling, men-in-kilts kind of place. It was downright dangerous. Murder and mayhem were a daily occurrence.

I don't know how long the Coupers lived in the borderlands or if they were in fact reivers, but I do know they were smugglers. In Scotland, whiskey dominates the story of smuggling. Starting in the 1600s, smuggling was standard practice in the area for 150 years. Most smugglers were also distillers and became ingenious at ways to avoid the whiskey taxman, by hiding the goods in caverns and underground tunnels in the hills and under private homes. It would be great if my ancestors were honest and noble, but whiskey isn't all bad.

Eventually the Coupers turned things around and became respectable. Instead of smuggling whiskey they became skilled barrel makers. They were also experts in the seasoning and forming of hard white oak that was used for shipbuilding. Some specialized as makers of weight-driven clocks for ships and buildings. According to a family member, one clock made by the Coupers still operates in the town square of St. Andrews, Scotland, today.

In the 1800s, Fredericks Couper's father, Thomas Smith Couper, was a captain of merchant sailing ships. Frederick's grandfather, William Couper, was a Master Mariner or Merchant Sea Captain, and operated a fleet of schooners that sailed to England and the Netherlands. His ships carried linen, flax, and jute fiber on their trade routes. According to census records, William listed a ship name as his address for over twenty years. I'm sure his family loved that. I wonder if sailing is in my ancestral DNA. For some reason I never get seasick. I once had a crazy trip crossing the English Channel on a ferry when there was a violent storm. The boat was tossed around pretty good. At one point the entire contents of the ship's dining room, dishes and all went flying on the floor and broke into pieces. Despite the rough sea, I only felt slightly off key, while others sat holding their stomachs.

A Mysterious Photo Appears

Unlike his father and grandfather, Frederick Couper had no interest in sailing. However, he was very creative and was a talented mural artist. I like to think that some of his artistic skills trickled down to Aunt Nan and me, since we are both artists.

While I was researching Frederick Couper, I became intrigued by a family photo Nan sent me, of three women and a child. In this photo, there's a severe-looking lady who is Frederick's grandmother. She is seated and is holding a small child. Two women are standing behind her. I couldn't stop looking at the photo. Something about it made want to know who these women were. They were dressed in fancy clothing and looked like they could be related. Nan couldn't find the original photo she emailed to me for some reason, but she remembered a couple of the names written on the back of it. She remembered that Alexandrina is the older lady seated, and the child on her lap was called Daisy. Nan was not sure who the two standing women were. Since the photo was missing, and I was learning mediumship, I decided to try and contact the women to see if they would tell me their names.

The mystery photo

I was excited to see what would happen. So far, I had only tried to contact specific people, but this time I was going to ask one or both of the two standing women in the photo to show up. I didn't know who would come forth, or if either of them would. This time, I decided to use a technique called automatic or inspirational writing, which is another psychic tool. Automatic writing is used for receiving written messages from spirits, guides, or other higher wisdom.

I sat quietly with pen in hand, and when I was ready, invited either woman to connect with me. With my eyes open, I began to receive impressions and words from a spirit, which I wrote down. The woman that came through identified herself as Mary.

The writing went as follows:

Mary is my christened name and I'm the woman on the left in the photo. I'm related to Alexandrina by marriage. Daisy is my child with James. James' father is an uncle to Frederick. With the men out to sea, the women in the family had to look after each other. The men were gone for long stretches of time, and no one watched what we were doing. We stayed together to raise children and care for the home.

This was interesting, since I didn't have a Mary or James on my radar. No one with those names was in the immediate family that I knew of. I decided to start by researching Mary, James, and Daisy to see if they were indeed connected to the photo. I ended up finding two families who could be matches.

One was a Mary (Langley) Couper married to a James Couper with a child named Daisy. They lived in Dundee, Scotland, which was the place the photo was taken. James Couper also worked as a marine engineer, which made sense as a possible connection, since the Coupers were sea captains. Their child, Daisy, was born in 1895, which works with the timing of this picture.

Secondly, I found in hand-written family history notes that there was a Mary and James Brown with a child named Margaret. A common nickname in that time for Margaret is Daisy, because the French version of the name "Marguerite" is also the French name for Oxeye Daisy. This family would be related somehow to Alexandrina Gordon Brown, the older lady seated in the photo, although at this point, I didn't know how.

Now what? I wasn't sure which Mary was the one who came through to me in the reading. And I wasn't able to find their exact connections to Frederick Couper, because the census records mostly listed ship names and crewmembers, rather than family names.

As I continued my research into the "Marys", I got an email from Nan, saying she thought maybe her mom, my grandmother Frances, was doing a bit of haunting in her house. Frances was Frederick and Annie's oldest daughter. She spent her last days in Nan's house before she died from cancer in 2002. Nan's son Ben had recently visited from Denver and was sleeping in the room where Frances died. While he was there, things kept going missing and would reappear a couple of days later, in plain sight. In this room, there was a suitcase filled with old photographs that were Frances' and this is where Nan kept the photo of the three ladies and Daisy. I was hoping she could look at the photo again to verify the names written on the back of it, but the photo was still missing. Nan couldn't find it anywhere. I wondered if it was my grandmother Frances or maybe Annie moving the photo around. Remember the spoon that fell from the wall display?

I decided to make a visit to Nan's house to look through the suitcase to see if I could help her locate the missing photo. On a cold fall day, I arrived at her house to find a big suitcase full of old letters and photos set on a table in the cozy living room. I was excited to get started, but before I began, Nan said, "Come in the hallway and check this out." The same old tarnished spoon that fell off the wall display previously was once again starting to fall off the wall! The display was recently repaired and was fine until that morning. Coincidence? I doubt it. I really felt my great-grandmother Annie was around and making her presence known. Maybe she was letting me know she was there to help.

I started to look through the many old pictures in the suitcase and found a much smaller version of the missing photo with names written on the back. Yay! It turned out the woman seated in the foreground was Alexandrina Gordon Brown, Frederick's grandmother, my third great-grandmother. The woman behind her on the right is Frederick's mother, Alexandrina Gordon Brown Couper. The child's name was listed as Daisy, but the woman on the left who I thought was Mary is named "Aunt Drina." What? The name Mary was not listed on the back of the photo. I was so disappointed! This meant my automatic writing was wrong and the spirit Mary was lying to me about being in the picture. I didn't expect this. A liar!

After further research, I was able to confirm that Aunt Drina was the third Alexandrina (Drina for short) in the photo. Her name is Alexandrina Gordon Black, one of Frederick's sisters. She was married to Richard Black. I didn't know there was a "Black" in the Couper line. The main clue in discovering this was found in Frederick's obituary. His two sisters are listed, one being a Mrs. Richard Black. Also listed in a hand-written death record I found in the suitcase are a Richard Black and his wife Alexandrina. Another quirk is the child's name Daisy is a nickname, not her birth name. I discovered that the Black's had two daughters, the eldest being named Alexandrina (nicknamed Daisy) and the other Winifred. This gives the photo meaning, as it would be a picture of four generations of Alexandrinas! One is Frederick's grandmother; one is his mother, one his sister, and lastly, his niece.

Alexandrina (Gordon) Brown (1822-1897)	→	Alexandrina Gordon (Brown) Couper (1848-1936)	→	Alexandrina "Drina" (Couper) Black (1868-1950)	→	Alexandrina "Daisy" Black (1893-1975)

Chart explaining the Alexandrinas

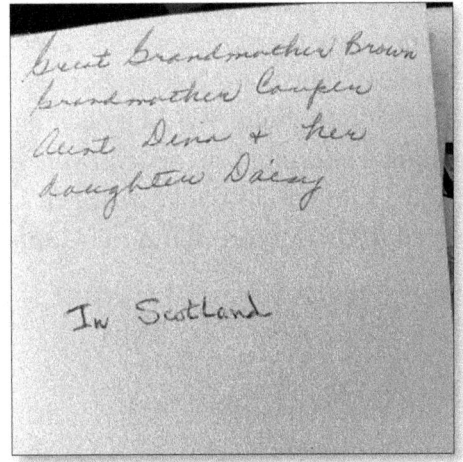

Writing on back of small picture of the Alexandrinas

Okay, great. Mystery solved. I now understood how the photo is connected to Frederick Couper's family. But why did a Mary talk to me and tell me she was in the picture? I love using psychic tools, but this is not a perfect science. You never know who may pop in and that's why asking for confirmation and evidence can be so important. It's interesting, however, that there are two potential families that fit the profile, both from the small town of Dundee, Scotland. This is amazing, really. I wondered which Mary came through hijacking my session. And, why didn't one of the Alexandrinas come through?

I decided to consult one of my mediumship teachers to get her opinion on why a spirit would lie to me. She agreed with me, that automatic writing isn't always foolproof. She said our imaginations may interfere with the workings. But how would my imagination have interjected a Mary into this? I didn't have any Mary on my mind. That name never came up in my research. She also said spirits wouldn't purposely mislead me, as Mary did. So why did she? Maybe she was a prankster.

Mary did give me some correct information about people who actually existed and could be my ancestors, but her name didn't fit with the photo I was asking about. Was Mary talking about another photo? The medium I consulted suggested that I can ask her for clarity on this. But I didn't feel I could trust her. I decided to let this go, and instead find out more about my Couper ancestors.

Borderlands marker stone. Photo credit: Dreamstime.com

A Mysterious Photo Appears

A whiskey barrel cooperage. A "Cooper " (Couper) is a barrel maker.

Photo Credit: Dreamstime.com

Family Tree for
The Couper Family
"The Sea Captains"

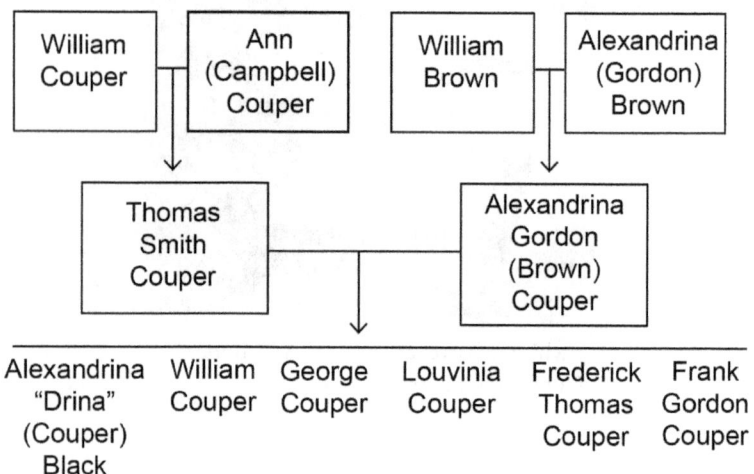

Other Couper Children that did not live to adulthood:
Susanna Couper (twin)
Ann Couper (twin)
Linnera Couper
Arthur Couper
Helen Couper
Leonerd Couper

Chapter 7
The Disappearance of Thomas Couper

When I was researching the Couper family, I had a vivid dream: I was on an old ship, a schooner with several massive sails. I looked down and could see my feet on a wooden deck. The ship was wide and full of ropes and riggings. The masts looked tall from the deck where I stood. When the waves hit, the ship creaked. I heard birds above and could smell the sea air. There was no one there but me. This dream was very clear and real. It made me think about what life would have been like for a sea captain before the age of steamers.

The timing of this dream was perfect. I was feeling stuck and thought I had already covered everything I could about the Coupers. There was limited written family history. The clarity of the dream inspired me to look closer at the ancestors who lived the seafaring life.

The Couper family were shipowners and merchant sea captains based in the town of Dundee, Scotland, in the 19th century. William Couper & Co. owned several ocean-going ships including schooners and square-rigged barks. William's son, Thomas Smith Couper, the father of my great-grandfather Frederick, captained his father's ships when he came of age.

Thomas' later life is a mystery. He was born in 1846 and died in 1934. Four of his children were the first Coupers to emigrate to the United States, including Frederick Couper. Thomas married in 1866, and later moved with his wife to a house on Logie St.

in Dundee. The census records showed this street address and, as was common for sea captains at the time, also showed ship names as addresses. 1901 is the last year Thomas appears on the census record for Dundee. He is missing from the 1911 census. Where did he go, I wondered.

It's unusual for a husband to be excluded on a census record if he was alive. This prompted me to want to dig a bit deeper. Since a census is conducted every ten years, many things could change in that time. Valuation or tax rolls were collected more often, so I started to investigate this.

Mysteriously, in 1915, Thomas showed up on tax rolls in the nearby town of Falkirk. This is puzzling because his wife Alexandrina continued to live in Dundee and is recorded on the 1911 census there. The tax rolls and census records confirm Thomas lived in Falkirk until his death in 1934. On his death record, he is listed as married to Margaret Bennett, yet there are no records of a divorce from his wife Alexandrina Brown Couper or of a marriage to Margaret Bennett.

On a British Genealogy website, I learned that a woman in England had also done research into this same Margaret Bennett, who was her great-grandaunt. The researcher was as perplexed as I was. None of the formal records found by me or Margaret's descendant confirm her identity as a wife to Thomas.

To deepen the mystery, in 1911 Alexandrina moved out of the family home and in with her daughter Alexandrina. By 1925, she had moved again to a modest flat on a narrow city street in Dundee. She is listed as a widow on tax rolls from 1925 to the time of her death in 1936. Thomas was alive and well in 1925. Did she think Thomas was dead? Did Thomas fake his death, or slip silently away? In family letters that his son Frank wrote in the 1970s, there is much about the Couper history in Scotland and in Dundee. But barely a mention of his father Thomas.

I was getting more curious about Thomas and what happened to him. The town of Falkirk is only 60 miles from Dundee. If Thomas were running away, he didn't go very far. Falkirk is near the port city of Grangemouth. Work as a seaman was available to him. In 1911, he was 65 years old. According to the other researcher, in Thomas's obituary, it says he has no family. I know for a fact he had quite a large family. When I find out things like this, my ancestors come to life. I sense their personalities and a story begins to unfold.

The marriage of Alexandrina and Thomas showed signs of trouble early on. After only two and a half years of marriage, Thomas posted this Intimation in the Dundee Courier:

I, the undersigned, do hereby intimate that I shall not be responsible for any debts contracted by my wife, Alexandrina Brown or Couper on or after this date, until further notice.
Thomas S Couper, Dundee, November 28, 1868

This is probably not the best way to begin a marriage.

I decided to investigate Thomas' history in Dundee to see what I could find. It's true, his life at sea kept him away from home. However, he did manage to father twelve children with Alexandrina. Six of the children died before reaching adulthood. I found this out by looking at death and census records. From 1851-1891, on the census, there were several children's names and ages listed. Then the names started disappearing from the records at intervals. One of the confirmed deaths was noted in a family letter. This was Arthur Couper, who accidentally drowned when he was a crew member on a ship. He was 17 years old.

I don't have death records for all the children, but according to Health in Scotland (1840-1940), the age group most vulnerable to death by illness was the very young. Children under ten accounted for more than half the deaths in parts of Scotland in the early 19th century. Diseases such as scarlet sever, tuberculous, and cholera were among the killers of the time. Two of the Couper girls died within one day of each other in December of 1889. One from consumption (TB) and the other from bronchitis at 9 months old. It was sad to see their older brother William was a witness on both of their death records. That must have been difficult for him. The remaining siblings, except their daughter Alexandrina and son William, emigrated to America between 1911 and 1920.

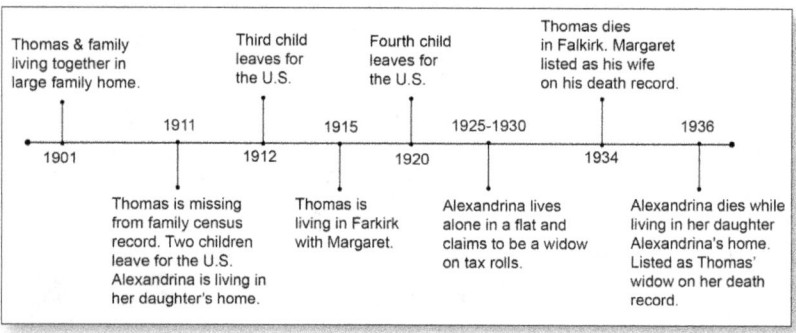

Thomas Couper timeline

I was curious to learn more about why four of the Couper children left Scotland for America, after Alexandrina's husband was gone. They were my great-grandfather Frederick, his older siblings George and Louvinia, and his youngest brother Frank. They all arrived separately and settled in different parts of the United States. For some reason, they didn't stick together. Frederick lived in Madison, Wisconsin, George near Boston in Dorchester, Massachusetts, Louvinia in Port Chester, New York, on Long Island Sound, and Frank in Tulsa, Oklahoma. There is no mention in the family stories or records of the three brothers ever returning to Scotland for a visit, or of their mother or sister ever visiting them, although Louvinia moved back to Scotland late in her life. Their brother William left Scotland but settled in England.

To understand why they left, I went back to learn more about their parents, the place they lived and its history in shipbuilding and ship ownership. I wanted to get a picture of what life was like for them in their growing up years.

Dundee is a coastal city on the Tay estuary that opens to the North Sea. It is Scotland's sunniest city and close to a beautiful countryside. It was a whaling port and a major shipbuilding town during the Couper children's growing up years and well into the 20th century. In Dundee, 2,000 sailing and steamer ships were built between 1871 and 1881 alone. The SS Californian was built in Dundee. This is the ship that my great-grandmother Annie sailed on to America after she missed boarding the Titanic.

The Californian was a freighter originally designed to carry cotton. When it was taken over by the White Star line it was able to accommodate passengers. There were 47 cabins. The cabins were affordable and comfortable for ordinary people leaving Europe for a new life in America. The facilities for passengers were similar to the second class of most ships of the time. Cabins had electric lighting which was not always the case on ships. There was a smoking room with oak paneling on the upper deck, plus a nicely decorated dining room for the guests. In 1912, the SS Californian was less than 20 miles from the Titanic when it radioed for help. Unfortunately, the wireless operator had gone to bed and missed the call.

From the mid-1800s to the early 1900s, there was fierce competition among ship builders in the British Isles. Everyone wanted to build the biggest, the best, and the unsinkable. Scotland had one of the world's largest and successful shipbuilding industries until the late 19th century.

At the Dundee docks, there were overcrowded tenements with rough conditions for the workers. However, the town also had its share of wealth. There were castles dating back to the 12th century and manor houses where the prosperous lived. Because my ancestors were shipowners and merchant seaman, they lived a good life. Some census records show street addresses, so I was able to look up a few of their homes in this time period. Many of these homes are still standing. It felt like I was spying, but Google Maps made it easy. In 1891, Thomas and Alexandrina and their family lived in a nice house in a well-kept neighborhood. Their house was a long two-story, with decorative brickwork and three chimneys. There was a terraced front garden with a low brick wall by the street. It still looks good today, so I can imagine it was even better in its day.

A merchant sea captain such as Thomas Couper would have needed to be a businessman, seaman and crew manager. The lifestyle would have been extremely hard on family life, especially for the wives. According to an article about sea history in the UK National Archives, the wives of sailors endured years of absence and uncertainty. They brought up the young children, managed domestic affairs and often took on more responsibility than other women whose husbands lived on land. There might only be a short break between the end of one voyage and the beginning of the next to spend time with their husbands. Plus, dealing with the death of several children would have been difficult if Thomas was gone.

I studied the history of several ships of that era. Many were damaged at sea, sunk, or sold, which could end a man's career abruptly on a particular ship. There were also many collisions. This seemed odd to me that two giant ships could run into each other, but weather was a factor. If it was misty and storming, without modern radar and lights, I could see how this could happen. And it did, often. The North Sea and the English Channel have long been known as one of the most dangerous places to sail.

If Thomas lost his ship, or his job as captain on a ship, this history could be a clue to what may have happened to him, his business, and his family. As WWI approached, the political tensions that led to the war mounted across Europe. Ships were requisitioned

The Disappearance of Thomas Couper

to be used for military purposes. This could coincide with Thomas leaving Dundee for Falkirk if he couldn't captain a merchant ship any longer. He was too old to join the Royal Navy. All commercial sailings were initially suspended in August of 1914, with the outbreak of the war. During the war, many ships were torpedoed and sunk in the English Chanel. Thomas most likely lost his main source of income in these years. And he was not a young man any longer.

It is difficult to know if Thomas was a shipowner along with being a captain when his father's company William Couper & Co was in business. William was retired as ship master by 1901 and ran a shop as a tobacconist and stationer (a person who sold fancy snuff and cigars). When he died in October of 1910, his probate record stated his estate was worth £144. That would be the equivalent of about $22,000 in 2024. According to the family letters, at some point, the Couper ships were sold to the Cunard line. The sale must have happened when William retired from being a ship's master, so the business was not passed on to Thomas. This was the first time in two or more generations that the Coupers did not have a guaranteed future in owning and captaining ships.

In William's will, money was left to Thomas, which was paid out in December of 1910. I wonder if Thomas took this as an opportunity to start over in another town without his wife. Also in the will, William listed three men as executors. All non-family members. They were instructed to use some of the funds to pay for his funeral and burial expenses. After a long and tedious search, I found no obituary, burial, or gravestone records for him. What did they do with poor William? He did have status as a retired sea captain and merchant in Dundee, so one would think he would have a gravesite somewhere.

Once Thomas arrived in Falkirk, he went to work as an ordinary seaman and warehouseman at an iron factory. Even though he was an older man at this time, he was not retired. And from the records, it appears that his wife thought he was dead. His children never mentioned him in family letters. It's not that shocking that a man would run off with another woman, but it is a mystery why his first wife was unaware that he was alive and living a short distance away, and why his assumed second wife was unaware that he was still married to someone else.

At this point, I thought I would see if Thomas was available in spirit. I often use my spirit guide Ivan when connecting with my ancestors (more on spirit guides in Chapter 17). Guides can help us to connect with the spirit realm. I imagined Ivan in his living room in New Orleans. He likes to have a glass of sherry sitting next to him, although he barely drinks it.

I asked Thomas to join us in the room. Moments later, I saw him in my mind's eye. He was a short man. He was dressed in a ship captain's uniform. Ivan poured sherry for us, but Thomas asked for whiskey. A tumbler was set next down next to him filled with amber liquid. To his right stood Margaret. She appeared as a small woman with dark hair and eyes. This scene may seem like it's my imagination, and in a way, it is. Imagination is a tool and opens a door that provides a pathway for psychic or mediumship connection. It works.

I thanked them for coming. I also told Thomas telepathically that I was not here to judge his actions. In my life, I also left my spouse because the situation was impossible. Thomas didn't elaborate but nodded in agreement. I asked him if he could help me find any more information about him, including his obituary. I looked extensively for it previously and could not find it. I know it existed, because the person who was researching Margaret Bennett referenced it in her findings. Thomas said I should look again, today. We finished our communication, and I sent him and Margaret away with gratitude and light. I appreciate that the ancestors come through for me.

A few minutes later, I went to my computer and went to the British Newspaper Archives website. I typed in the same search term criteria I used a few times before when looking for Thomas. In my previous attempts, nothing came up, but this time his obituary popped up immediately.[1] I verified this was Thomas Couper my ancestor by the dates mentioned and other clues. This felt like magic or perhaps the help of my ancestor.

It's not what is included in the obituary, but instead what is missing that confirms the theory that he was hiding from his family. The obituary mentions his 45 years of being a sea captain, but does not say it was in Dundee, which it was. There is also no mention of his father's ships. It does reference the fact that he was a seaman on the Carron (Iron) Company ships near Falkirk. The Carron Company ran its own shipping line and produced munitions during both World Wars. It says he is survived by a widow, with no mention of her name. No children names are mentioned. He "had no family," according to the obituary.

If his "widow" Margaret posted the obituary in the Dundee paper, she likely had no idea of the extent of his former life, family, or wife. I wondered if his real wife Alexandrina read it. It was not posted in the Falkirk paper, as far as I could tell. I searched for it more than once. Two years later, in 1936, Alexandrina's short obituary was posted in the Dundee newspaper. It mentions she is the widow of Thomas and only mentions one child, her daughter, Alexandrina Gordon Black, whom she lived with at the end of her life. It is interesting that none of the other Couper children were included in her obituary either. I asked Nan if anyone in her family ever talked about Thomas Couper, and she doesn't recall they did.

It seems that the Couper family fell apart in Scotland. I decided to move on from researching Thomas and learn about the lives of the four children and their lives in America.

---

[1] *Dundee Evening Telegraph,* (1934)

Death of Mr Thomas Couper

The death of Mr Thomas Couper, a native of Lochee, has taken place at his residence, Thistle Street, Falkirk.

Mr Couper was born in Dundee 87 years ago, and 45 years was a seaman, taking his master's certificate for foreign-going vessels in 1900. In 1914 he left the sea and was employed as a warehouseman in the Falkirk Iron Company's foundry, which position he held until six years ago, when he retired.

Despite his advanced years, Mr Couper took an active interest in affairs, and could remember the many eventful happenings when he sailed from the port of Grangemouth in the Carron Company's ships. He is survived by a widow, and had no faimly.

Obituary for Thomas Smith Couper

The SS Californian. The ship Annie sailed on to America. Contributor: GL Archive/Almay Stock Photo

Portrait of the Four Alexandrinas

- Alexandrina, Fred's Sister
- Alexandrina, Fred's Mother, Thomas's Wife
- Alexandrina, Fred's Grandmother
- Alexandrina, (Daisy), Daughter of Fred's sister Alexandrina

Portrait of the Four Alexandrinas

Chapter 8
The Coupers in America

The story of Thomas Couper and his family is perplexing. For whatever reason Thomas left his wife and moved to another town. And no one seemed to know about it. Another curiosity about the Couper family was a listing I found in a local Dundee paper.[1] This was posted by William Couper (Thomas' father), looking for his father, John Couper.

Missing Friends:

The family of John Couper-last heard of at Shotts Ironworks. Would they write to William Couper, 33 Paton's Lane, Dundee?

John Couper would have been around 86 years old in 1892, when the query was posted. Who knows if he was even alive then, but William was looking for any of the family members.

The town of Shotts is in North Lanarkshire, Scotland. Shotts Ironworks was established in 1802 and was a major iron works. It was built to take advantage of the large reserves of ironstone found in the area. The local population worked in the iron works and the associated coal mines. If John Couper was living in Shotts, he most likely earned a living there at the Iron works.

This answered a question about who started the shipping business and when the first Coupers became ship masters. This was a

---

[1] *Dundee People's Journal,* (August of 1892)

bit disappointing to me. I envisioned a long line of ship captains. Instead, it must have started with William Couper. After all, pirate blood ran in his veins, an ancestral connection to sailing. This may be a bit of a stretch, but I like it.

By the looks of things, the Couper family seemed to go their own ways with little communication with each other. When Thomas' wife Alexandrina died, her obituary only mentioned her eldest daughter, whom she lived with. Not any of her other children. I imagine Alexandrina Black was responsible for posting her mother's obituary. She only mentioned that her mother was the widow of T.S. Couper and beloved mother of Mrs. Richard Black (herself). I don't think cost was an issue. Like her parents, she and her husband lived in a nice home and looked to be doing well in life. Maybe it was because the rest of her siblings left the country and left her to take care of their mother. In any case, I found it peculiar, but they wouldn't be the first family to be at odds with each other.

The first Couper child to leave Scotland was my great-grandfather, Frederick (Fred). He arrived in New York in March of 1911, at the age of 29. On his paperwork, he is described as short and slender and having brown hair and eyes. He weighed only 122 pounds. I found physical descriptions on all the immigration records for the Couper siblings. It's funny to me that each person's looks were assessed this way. Although, when my great-grandmother Annie McIntosh arrived in 1912 from Scotland, to join Fred, I didn't see any reference to her looks on her paperwork. For anyone doing ancestry work, this kind of detail is nice when it's included. It really helps to get a feel for what my ancestors looked like since I don't have photos for many of them.

Fred and Annie settled in Madison, Wisconsin. As I mentioned, Fred was an artist and worked as a decorator and indoor painter. He did projects for private homes and businesses, including murals. Annie and Fred had three daughters, one being my maternal grandmother Frances. As a couple, they lived an active life. Long before social media existed, there was the society page in the local paper. I found several listings of dinners at their home, parties for their kids, trips they took and visits from family.

Fred died after a long illness at 53 years old. On the one-year anniversary of his death, my great-grandmother Annie posted this poem in the Madison newspaper:[2]

In Memoriam:

In memory of my beloved husband Fred Couper, who died June 28, 1935:

Loving and kind in all his ways,
Upright and just to the end of his days.
Sincere and true in his heart and mind,
Beautiful memories he left behind.

Annie lived another 24 years without Fred. She had to give up their house and went to live with their daughter in Iowa, and later in Milwaukee with my grandmother Frances. It makes me sad to think Annie braved the ocean voyage to follow Fred to America, only to have their love story end with his untimely death.

The second Couper to sail to America was Louvinia (Lacy) Mary McGill Couper in December of 1911, eight months after Fred had arrived. She was 32 years old at the time. On the ship manifest, she is described as 5' 2", weighing 110 pounds, with a birthmark on her face. Louvinia first traveled to Toronto, Canada, to stay with a friend for a while. By 1920, she lived in Connecticut and later in the village of Port Chester, New York, where she took a job as a governess. During the years she was there, the Depression hit. Luckily, if she was working for a wealthy family, she would have been taken care of.

---

[2] *Wisconsin State Journal (1935)*

I felt bad for Louvinia. Her brothers lived in different parts of the country and pursued their dreams. She, on the other hand, probably took one of the only jobs available to her at the time. She set sail back to Scotland in 1951, forty years after she arrived. She was 73 years old. On the ship manifest, it lists her stay back in Scotland as "indefinite." It's interesting that she didn't stay on and live with one of her brothers in America.

Louvinia died in 1963 in Dundee, Scotland, in the same house her mother Alexandrina died in, owned by her sister Alexandrina's family. Her death record states she was single. I don't see any evidence that she ever married. She died from a virus infection at 84 years old.

George Couper and his wife Grace arrived in New York, May of 1912. He was 37 years old, and his description includes his height of 5'4", brown hair and a fresh complexion. He was fairly short and so were Fred and Louvinia. Frederick's daughter, my grandmother Frances, wasn't even 5 feet tall. And I am 5' 2". The Coupers could be the reason for our small stature.

George settled in Dorchester, near Boston. He went to work for a company called Berwick Cake Company as an accountant, the same occupation he had had in Dundee. Berwick claims to be the first to invent the Whoopie Pie. However, there are several baking companies that claim they were also the first. A Whoopie pie is described as two round-shaped pieces of chocolate cake with a creamy filling. I've never had the desire to try one. Sometime between 1920 and 1930, George became Vice President of the company. Nice work, George!

For a few reasons, I feel a kinship with Frank Couper, the youngest sibling. In 1920, he sailed for New York, at the age of 28, after serving in the Royal Air Force in WWI. Once there, he took up residence at the Chelsea Hotel. I was excited to find this out. It's one of my favorite places. At the time, the Chelsea was accepting short-term visitors, as it had been converted into an apartment-hotel combination. After its renovation in 2022, I was lucky to have drinks in the beautiful lobby bar and then dinner in the restaurant. I felt the vibe of all the famous artists, writers, and musicians, such as Patti Smith and Leonard Cohen, who once lived there. When Frank was a resident of the Chelsea, one of the bottom floors was leased to the Greater Engineering Company. Frank was an engineer, so that may have been why he was staying there.

Sometime in the 1920s, Frank moved to Tulsa, Oklahoma. That's a switch from New York. By 1928, Frank was married to Marjorie Mae Voordees. They were married in a Unitarian church. I love this, it shows open-mindedness. Unitarians welcome the diversity of various belief systems. In my life, I've attended many lectures at Unitarian churches.

Sometime in the 1930s, Frank became the owner of a surgical supply company named Frank G. Couper, Inc. He designed surgical suites for Hillcrest Medical Center and St. John Medical Center in Tulsa. This is quite an accomplishment. He was also a founding member of the Tulsa Scottish Club. I know he did well financially. Nan once visited him in 1960 on the way to Californian. She said he lived in a fantastic house full of Scottish artifacts. I would love to have seen it.

In September of 1940, all men between 18 and 64 years old were required to register for the WWII draft. I found the draft card for Frank, and it lists his description as 5'3" (another shorty), brown hair and blue eyes, burn scars on both hands and a wound scar above one eye. I wonder if this could be from injuries from WWI. As it turned out, only men 18 to 45 were drafted. This meant Frank was too old to serve in another World War.

The thing I find the most intriguing about Frank is his status as a high-ranking Freemason. I've read several books on the Freemasons. Many famous people were members, including many of our founding fathers. I was surprised to find that Frank wasn't the only Freemason in the family. In the obituary for Frank's brother, George, it states that he joined the Gate of the Temple Lodge, in Dorchester, Massachusetts, in 1921. That sounded like a Mason lodge to me, so I looked it up. Yes, it is! Two brothers living in separate parts of the country were Freemasons, wow. However, it is said no two Masonic lodges are the same. Each has a unique personality driven by their members. The lodge was a place for dinners, events, and just plain hanging out. Freemasonry involves secret rituals often with age-old artifacts, art, and pageantry. Perhaps that's why Frank had so many artifacts in his home.

I later found the U.S. Mason membership card for George Couper on an ancestry website. The card shows that George was also a Freemason in Scotland long before moving to the U.S. He belonged to the Caledonian Lodge #254 in Dundee, Scotland. The lodge was on the same street as William Couper's tobacco shop. I wonder if William was also a Freemason. In William's will, he left his silver watch with gold Albert chain to his grandson George. The Albert chain could signify a club membership. Or it could simply be a sea captain's watch chain. It stands out that William left a personal item to George. No one else in his will was left any item other than money.

Dundee had a total of seven Masonic lodges. The Caledonian Lodge dates to 1814. In Scottish Rite Freemasonry, degrees teach a series of moral lessons culminating in the 32nd degree, Master of the Royal Secret. I would love to know the Royal Secret. I must admit I'm nosy about what goes on in a Masonic lodge.

I decided to do some spirit communication with my great-granduncle Frank. I don't always use Ivan my guide to facilitate spirit communication, but this time, I did. Ivan appeared in my mind's eye in his New Orleans living room. Since it was morning, he served chicory coffee and beignets instead of glasses of sherry. In the spirit world, powdered sugar stays put, so it wasn't messy.

After greeting Ivan, I invited Frank Couper to join us. He arrived telepathically, dressed in a beige three-piece suit. He was not tall, (as confirmed by his draft card), with light brown hair, glasses, and a mustache. I asked him if there was anything he could share with me about his life. He showed me a book. It was thick, bound, with handwritten pages and illustrations. At this time, I wasn't sure of its meaning, but later realized Frank wrote accounts of family history, which I have referred to often. We spent a few more minutes together, then I asked him to share a Freemason secret with me. I couldn't help myself.

I knew I was asking a lot, but it didn't hurt to try. He said, *"Your recent training with Uri Geller has taught you to use your mindpower. This is a similar practice the Masons use in ritual to manifest positive outcomes in our lives and for others."* This is a good insight from my ancestor. I had just completed a Master Class with the famous psychic Uri Geller. I appreciated Frank's message. I can't find any evidence that Frank was a Freemason in Scotland like George, but it makes sense that he could have been.

Because the Couper children all lived apart in the U.S., I was curious if Frank or the other Couper siblings ever visited one another. Once again in the society pages of the Madison newspaper, I got my answer. In 1922, Frank traveled to Madison to visit Fred, and meet Annie for the first time. He never knew her in Scotland. After that, Frank, and their brother George, visited Madison a few times before Fred's death in 1935. There is no mention of Louvinia ever traveling to Wisconsin.

I had a visit of my own. It was a cold crisp day in March. My partner Joe and I were in Madison for a conference and the next day was free, so we decided to drive over to Forest Hill Cemetery where Annie and Fred Couper were buried. We didn't know the location of the graves, but armed with the section number, we drove the curvy cemetery roads to look for them. We made our way towards the back of the place to find Section 11. Once there, we got out of the car and split up. We walked up and down the rows to look for their graves. There had been a heavy rain the day before, so the ground was soggy and muddy. We strolled slowly, taking in all the names of the people buried there. Some graves dated to the early 1800s. There is something calming about walking in a cemetery. At least during daylight hours.

After a while, we weren't having any luck and Joe needed to make a phone call. He went back to our car and was gone for about half an hour. Alone, I continued to walk up and down the aisles under the tall trees. My fashionable yet impractical leather boots were full of mud and the wind was piercing. At one point, I said out loud, "Okay, Fred and Annie you're not making this easy!" Moments later, I located their graves. Flat grave markers, side by side. I stood at the foot of them and enjoyed the silence, except for a few loud crows overhead. It somehow felt good to stand there, knowing that beneath my feet were their bones. They became more real to me. I never met them in life, yet I'm telling their stories.

Later, I found out Nan knew where their graves were and could have told me where to look. I never thought to ask her. They were buried in a section of the cemetery designated for the Scottish community. Despite the mud, I was glad to have discovered their graves on my own.

That same day, we drove to the neighborhood in Madison where Fred and Annie previously owned a house. We located the bungalow style home, now overgrown with trees obscuring the front of it. It's charming and is just big enough for them to have raised their daughters. I felt sorry for Annie having to give up the house after Fred died.

The physical descriptions of the Couper children helped me to imagine them to some degree. I also have a clearer picture of Frank Couper from the mediumship session. In a way, I got to know

The Coupers in America

them all. The sea captains, the Alexandrinas, and the adventurous children of Thomas Couper.

Frank Couper's business in Tulsa, Oklahoma, 1938. He is standing somewhere by the storefront. Photo courtesy of Tulsa Historical Society & Museum

Inside Masonic lodge temple, location unknown. Contributor: GL Archive/Almay Stock Photo

Chelsea Hotel sign [left]. The author in front of the hotel in 2014.

Family Tree for Brown & Hay Families (Poorhouse Alexandrina)

Note: This is not a complete family tree

(c) H van den Berg-Cameron
Morayshire former workhouse site from the south, date unknown.
© H. van den Berg-Cameron.

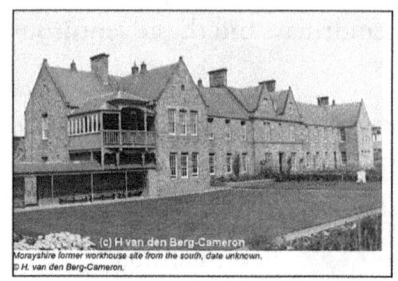

Morayshire Union Poorhouse
Photo Courtesy of Kam van den Berg

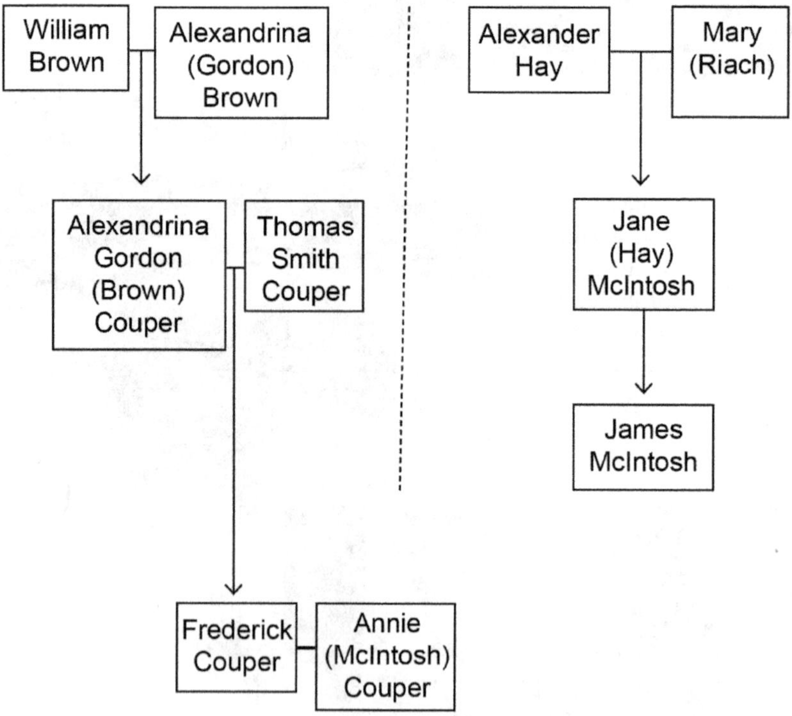
William Brown
Alexandrina (Gordon) Brown
Alexandrina Gordon (Brown) Couper
Thomas Smith Couper
Frederick Couper
Annie (McIntosh) Couper
Alexander Hay
Mary (Riach)
Jane (Hay) McIntosh
James McIntosh

Chapter 9
Poorhouse Alexandrina

We've all heard some variation of the phrase "Be careful or you'll end up in the poorhouse." My search of death records led me to believe that two of my ancestors died in poorhouses in Scotland: Alexandrina (Gordon) Brown, whose daughter married into the Couper family, and Mary Hay, whose daughter married into the McIntosh family. Both women ended up in poorhouses after their husbands died. Mary's husband Alexander didn't die in the poorhouse but was listed as a pauper on this death record. He received "outdoor relief" in the form of small weekly payments allotted to paupers but lived in his home.

The words poorhouse and pauper really bothered me. The thought of my ancestors spending their last years in a poorhouse brought up familiar feelings of lack. I was raised in a family that never seemed to have money. We weren't poor by some standards, but as kids, we didn't have much. My dad worked all the time, but constant bills from my mom's long hospital stays added up. She was often in mental health facilities for months at a time. And, in my dad's own words, "I drank all my money."

There were five of us. My parents, my sister, my brother, and me. From the age of ten through my teens, we lived in a three-bedroom apartment. My dad couldn't afford to buy a house. When I was growing up, dinners could be sparse, with no extras. We often bought our clothes and winter coats at the local Goodwill store. As a high school kid, I remember being relieved in the 1970s when it was in style to wear old Army jackets and beat-up frayed blue jeans. It didn't cost much to be hip in those days.

I graduated from high school when I was 17 years old and went to work immediately. My divorced father wasn't willing to support me any longer. Working three retail jobs at a time, I was able get an apartment with two other girls. As a young person, I lived on the edge. College wasn't an option at the time. Today, I am living a happy life full of love, travel, and adventure and I feel very lucky. But I was saddened to learn my ancestors called a poorhouse home in their later years. I remember how I felt growing up. Life was so uncertain.

Alexandrina Brown died in the Arbroath-St. Vigeans Combination Poorhouse, near Dundee, Scotland, in 1897. Her cause of death is listed as "burns." When I located this record, I reread the cause of death a few times, thinking maybe I wasn't seeing the word correctly. But it is hand-written clearly in black ink. Later, I found a newspaper article[1] that confirmed she died from a burning accident at the poorhouse. Her husband William had died two years before this in 1895, and she was admitted to Arbroath-St. Vigeans after his death.

Mary Hay lived in Morayshire Union Poorhouse at Bishopsmill in Elgin, Scotland, in 1870, after her husband Alexander died. She lived there for only two months before she also died. Perhaps she was admitted to the poorhouse while still in mourning. The cause of her death is listed as old age.

Both women were widowed and most likely ill or suffering the normal ailments of old age when they entered the poorhouse. I wondered why their own families wouldn't have taken care of them in their homes. Surely someone could look after them.

---

[1] *Dundee Courier*, (1897)

People from the poorhouse, and other paupers, were often buried in unmarked graves. Sometimes several people would be buried in one gravesite, because they were poor. I decided to learn about the poorhouses of Scotland.

The Morayshire Poorhouse where Mary lived was brand new in 1864. It was a large institutional brick building with two wings, one for women and one for men. In the men's and women's dormitories, rows of single beds lined a big room on two sides. In this cheerless room, all the beds looked the same, with a chamber pot beneath each. Chamber pots had the nickname goesunder because they were kept under a bed. They were also called pisspots. They were used by everyone because there was no indoor plumbing. The poorhouses of this time did not have toilets or shared outhouses, there were no common sewers. There was also a lack of privacy in these barren rooms. No frills whatsoever.

On the women's side of the house there were various work and utility rooms, including a laundry. A large dining hall and chapel were located on one end of the building. The women had an outdoor space called the yard, and there was a separate yard for the men. If a person was able to work, they would be assigned duties. Mary and Alexandrina were most likely too ill to have duties.

The residents of poorhouses were called inmates. They were a diverse lot. There were the old and sick, vagrants, paupers, mentally ill (labeled lunatics), disabled persons, and women who were pregnant with illegitimate children. There was a Lunacy Board that decided if a mentally ill person qualified to be a resident. And every person who came to the poorhouse had to be approved by the Parochial Board set up by the local parishes. People couldn't just show up and live there. Poorhouses were run by a Governor and a Matron, who were often a married couple. The Governor and the Matron each had their own set of responsibilities. If an inmate was disorderly, the Governor could punish the person by adding extra hours to his or her work schedule and withhold food and drink for two or three days. This seems harsh, but they were trying to control and manage a lot of people.

One governing couple in the town of Elgin took it upon themselves to make the poorhouse they ran more pleasant.[2] They added bright curtains to the rooms, fresh flowers, bowls of fruit and rugs on the floors, plus were kindly and compassionate to the inmates.

In general, conditions were not perfect in the poorhouses; however, the benefit of free medical care was very important. In newspaper article[3], a Mr. Hughes says, "The poorhouse is the dearest place any pauper could be sent to." The alternative was being homeless and begging for money or food. The earliest acts of the Scottish parliament that address relief for the poor date from 1424. Between that time and the early 1800s, there were many poor relief systems put in place. Many poorhouses were built after the 1845 Scottish Poor Law Act was created. They were not government funded. Money to run the poorhouses was raised by churches, from private individuals, fees from baptisms, marriages and burials, and other fee collections and charities. Often people donated clothing, shoes, food, and even snuff. In many ways the Scottish people were leaders in poor relief in their day.

I found several local newspaper articles[4] from the mid 1800s that discussed the proper care and consideration of the poor. The town citizens were very concerned about how the poor were treated. Some opposed the poorhouse, saying it was no better than a prison, but the majority believed it was better than living and someday dying in the streets without regular food or medical care.

---

[2] *Willie and Isabella Cameron, Elgin, Scotland*
[3] *Dundee Courier, (1800s)*
[4] *Aberdeen Journal, (1868)*

Like other new inmates, when my ancestors first arrived at the poorhouse they were asked to change into a uniform or specified type of standard clothing, and to give up any personal belongings. This would be hard to do. Maybe there were cherished keepsakes that were taken away from them, at least for the time being. The women wore dresses made from a coarse fabric like mohair or wool. Itchy! And white caps for their heads, aprons, thick stockings, and woven slippers. A sense of style or uniqueness was out of the question. The clothing issued was meant to give everyone equal status and it was a way to identify the inmates if they left the property to do a little exploring around town. The clothes a person originally arrived in would be washed and put away, along with personal items, until they left or died. Inmates could leave at any time if they had a change in fortune or for any other reason.

The food in a poorhouse could be of poor quality because rats and mice would often get into the food supply. A typical meal consisted of oatmeal, cheese, and bread. Oatmeal is not my favorite, so I sympathize. Oats were introduced to Scotland by the ancient Romans. Scottish oats are produced in a way that gives them a smooth texture, like traditional porridge. According to National Geographic, archaeologists believe that oats were grown with other edible crops, yet they were rarely used for human consumption. I rest my case. In the poorhouse, oatmeal was an easy meal to serve a large group of people.

The water supply was considered unfit for drinking, so watered-down beer was served daily, along with buttermilk and tea. Many poorhouses had breweries and made their own beer. For meals, there was soup made with carrots, turnips, and bone broth, but almost no meat was served. Rabbits were donated by the local townspeople for "meat days." If a person was sick, the onsite medical officer could dispense wine, spirits, or other cordial as medicine. Anytime someone complained of an ailment, they could get a dram of whiskey. There were probably people lined up daily at the medic's door. Every year, there was a Christmas dinner and celebration for the inmates. This broke up the monotony of the usual fare. But the rest of the year, the lack of healthy food resulted in many cases of malnutrition.

I found a photo of a women's dining hall in a poorhouse. Row after row of women all wearing the same dresses, crammed into long tables. No one was smiling or looking at the others. All stared straight ahead or down at their plates.

In our time, we have nursing homes or other facilities where our loved ones can be taken care of by medical professionals, if families are no longer capable of doing this, can't afford it, or choose not to. Poorhouses had free medical care. There were hospital wards with trained medical and nursing staff. They took care of the elderly and sick at a time when there were few hospitals in rural areas. Poor health could be the main reason my ancestors ended up there. However, it still baffles me why two people with so many family members came to live in poorhouses.

Alexander Hay, husband of Mary, was a crofter, and leased a small croft or farm. He worked the land, which as he got older must have proved difficult. I'm sure he kept the farm going as long as he could. He died at home, and then Mary became a resident of the Morayshire Poorhouse. It was odd to me that their daughter Jane Hay didn't take her in. Jane seemed prosperous enough since she had a servant, my 2nd great-grandmother, Eliza. Jane was widowed and the head of her own household at the time, yet Mary didn't move into her home or into another family member's home.

Alexandrina Brown was a widow when she went to live in the Arbroath Poorhouse. Her husband is listed as deceased on her death record. His former occupation is given as a tailor and she as a laundress. They may have lived a comfortable life. So why would she end up a pauper, to be buried in an unmarked grave?

But the more I thought about these two women, who "ended up in the poorhouse," it suddenly hit me that it wasn't just my ancestor's fate, but also my mom's. Although different. When I was growing up, my mom's mental illness made it impossible for her to hold a job. In her last years, she lived in a public housing complex. She had no choice. My siblings and I were not equipped to take care of her financially or emotionally. She had to rely on social programs and the goodwill of others to survive, along with government-funded rent and health insurance.

Her apartment was like an oversized hospital room. Cold and unwelcoming with old linoleum floors. Every sound echoed. It was a bit like living in a tin can. The building's residents were mostly disabled and elderly people who were visited regularly by health care and social workers. My mom's mental health challenges didn't show from the outside, so the other residents treated her like she was a freeloader. It was depressing, to say the least. This is where she took her own life. I realized my mom's circumstances contributed to why the discovery of Alexandrina and Mary's time in the poorhouse is so upsetting to me. My research is helping me uncover the ancestral patterns of trauma with some of the women in my family.

In learning about my ancestors, I use conventional methods of ancestry research to find out what I can. And, as I've done previously when I get stumped, I then try mediumship. Poorhouse records are rare and hard to find. Especially personal details of the inmates. I wanted a bit more information, so I decided to ask my spirit guide Ivan to help me contact the two women.

For this mediumship session, I sat quietly and envisioned myself in Ivan's living room in New Orleans. In my mind's eye, I noticed the room was decorated with welcoming plush couches, full of pillows. A fire was burning in the grate, candles were lit, and sherry had been poured into glasses. One for each of us. In addition to Ivan and me, I invited the two women who were in the poorhouse, Alexandrina Brown and Mary Hay, and Mary's pauper husband Alexander Hay, the crofter. In my vision, Alexander and Mary arrived first. They sat together on a couch by the fireplace.

Alexander was tall and thin, wearing a rustic shirt and black overcoat. Mary was much shorter than him, and giggly. She looked up at him and seemed happy to be with him. Mary told me telepathically that she went to the poorhouse after Alexander died because she was sick. She said her children would visit her and bring her blankets. Alexander got up from the couch and went to the fireplace to stoke the fire. He appreciated the warmth. Scotland was cold and damp and he is forever trying to warm up. Mary showed me her left hand. It looked like something was wrong with it. Her thumb looked disjointed. I wondered if it was from arthritis.

Alexandrina joined us. Although she lived in Scotland at the same time as the Hays, as far as I know she was not known to them. She appeared to me as she would have looked in her youth, with long blond hair, with the sides pinned away from her face. She was wearing a long dress. I noticed she had high cheekbones. She carried a wicker basket with a handle. In it were several folded cloth dinner napkins. This was a clue.

As you may remember, when I use mediumship, I look for personal facts from the spirits that can be verified, such as how they looked in life. But this session ended without any real evidence or information about their families or why they were paupers. However, in the way that they appeared to me, their height, their clothing, Alexander being cold, their happiness about being together, Mary's hand, and the basket, they gave me a glimpse of their lives.

It was good to make this connection with the spirits, but something was nagging at me. One of the things about using psychic skills and mediumship is learning to trust one's intuition. I kept feeling a nudge to look again at my records about William and

Alexandrina Brown. Ancestors are people and they are still around us, so the feeling wouldn't go away. One day I heard telepathically, "If you're going to write about us, get it right."

This is where the story of my two women ancestors in the poorhouse took a turn. I decided to look more closely at the death record I found for Alexandrina Brown. On my second review, I noticed a few things that didn't fit. The first was Alexandrina's husband William's occupation, and the second was Alexandrina's maiden name. I then realized she was a different Alexandrina Brown. As it turns out, there were two couples named Alexandrina and William Brown who lived in the same county of Forfar. Also, both Alexandrinas died in 1879. The Alexandrina who died in the poorhouse was not my ancestor after all. Her maiden name was Bain. My ancestor's maiden name was Gordon.

Alexandrina (Bain) Brown (Laundress)	William ____ Brown (Tailor)	Alexandrina (Gordon) Brown (Wife)	William ____ Brown (Ship's Carpenter)
Married Couple Not my ancestors		Married Couple My ancestors	

Chart showing the two Alexandrinas

Alexandrina's husband's occupation as a tailor didn't feel like it matched what I found in my research about my ancestor William Brown. To check this, I dug back into my records and reviewed several census records. According to these records, my ancestor William's occupation is a "joiner" and "ship's wright," not a tailor. A joiner is a woodworker or carpenter, and a ship's wright helped construct and build ships by creating wooden parts. As a ship's carpenter, he sailed with the ship to fix things as needed on the voyage. This indicated that I had found the death record for a different Alexandrina Brown. The woman who appeared to me as a young lady with blond hair and died a pauper must be Alexandrina (Bain) Brown.

I was upset to have made this mistake, but instead of tossing "Poorhouse Alexandrina" out of the story, I decided to include her, even though she is not part of the family tree. Like my ancestor Mary Hay, she ended up in the poorhouse at the end of her life. It must have been a shock to both to give up the comfort of their homes and go to a public institution which was so stark and unforgiving. I'm sure they had no choice.

I have some fear about this myself. I have no children of my own. No one is obligated to take care of me in my old age, even though I have a loving partner. And I'm surrounded by friends and family who would. This feeling is not logical, and I try not to dwell on it, but these thoughts lurk somewhere in my subconscious.

I realize that when I connected with these three people using mediumship, they gave me clues about themselves that I cannot prove are true. Although Alexandrina (Bain) Brown did show me clean and folded cloth napkins that could be a symbol for laundry or laundress, which was her occupation. When I called on these spirits, I asked for the women who had been in the poorhouse to show up, not knowing that one of them was not my ancestor.

For me this is a lesson in trust. I've had previous success with mediumship, where spirits gave me information that was later verified immediately by the person I was reading for. Because of this success, I'm less likely to question what the three spirits showed to me in the session with Ivan. As my training evolves, I'm learning to believe in what the deceased person is giving me in the form of images and telepathic communication. Perhaps this can become a form of evidence that I can rely on.

My ancestor Alexandrina (Gordon) Brown was part of a previous mystery about the identities in the photo of three women and a baby called Daisy. She is my third great-grandmother and is the oldest of the three seated in the foreground, with Daisy on her lap. Later, I discovered that she was also widowed when she died and lived with relatives at the time. But she did not go to the poorhouse.

In the mediumship session, Alexander and Mary Hay were reunited and looked happy to be together. In the afterlife, Mary is not suffering from poverty or illness. Neither is Alexandrina (Bain) Brown. They are no longer in the poorhouse.

Example of a women's dining hall in a workhouse [poorhouse]. Contributor: History and Art Collection/ Almay Stock Photo

Example of a chamber pot. Contributor: Dreamstime Stock Images

Sylvon Blair

Family Tree for Sylvon Blair
My grandfather
Note: This is not a complete family tree

```
┌─────────────┐   ┌──────────────┐
│ John Blair  │───│    Eliza     │
│             │   │  (Pearson    │
│             │   │  Cocheran)   │
│             │   │    Blair     │
└─────────────┘   └──────────────┘
        │
        ▼
  Alexander Blair
        │
        ▼
   William Blair
        │
        ▼
   Samuel Blair
        │
        ▼
  ┌──────────────┐     ┌──────────────┐
  │ Theodore     │─────│ Mary Adeline │
  │   Blair      │     │   (Blair)    │
  │              │     │    Blair     │
  └──────────────┘     └──────────────┘
         │
         ▼
  Francis Marion Blair
         │
         ▼
   Ernest Tiley Blair
         │
         ▼
     Sylvon Blair
```

Clan Blair's motto is "Amo Probos" which means, "I Love the Virtuous."
The Blairs can be traced to the 1200s in Scotland.

Pendant above from celticstudio.com

Chapter 10

Stories of the Blairs

In one of my mediumship classes, we split into small groups and practiced giving readings for each other. A classmate spoke up and said she had a message for me. An older man was coming through. She said he died suddenly of a heart attack. He loved nature, gardening, dogs, owned a boat and liked to fish. Then she said, "His dog remembers you and how you helped him."

Wow! From her description of the man, I knew this was my grandfather Sylvon Blair. And to have his dog come through was unexpected. It gave me chills.

My grandfather died of a heart attack while sitting on a pier and fishing in Lake Michigan, in Northern Wisconsin. He was only 62 years old. I was in high school at the time and was shaken by his death for two reasons. It was my first experience with anyone close to me dying and he was one of my favorite people. I have a vivid memory of his funeral, the first one I ever attended. I sat in the front row during the service with a view of the open coffin. Before the memorial service started, two old women approached the coffin. I was horrified as one of the women lifted my dead grandfather's hand and started yanking on a ring he wore on his finger. She pulled and pulled, trying to remove the ring. The funeral director finally ran over and stopped her. The woman wanted to get his jewelry before the coffin was closed, but she could have arranged to do this in private. The women were related to my grandfather's second wife, Peg, my step-grandmother. This scene was forever burned into my memory.

I prefer to remember my grandfather Sylvon as a man who always encouraged me to do well in school and had lots of interests and hobbies. I loved visiting with him as a kid. He taught himself geology and would show me his rock collection, which over the years he'd polished into shiny colorful stones. He also collected Native American arrowheads he found in the woods and near Wisconsin lakes. Sylvon played guitar, but couldn't sing. I must have inherited this from him because I can't sing a note! He knew a lot about Wisconsin local history and lore. I grew up in a crazy, unstable household, but when I visited my grandfather, I felt some peace and stability. He would sit in his big leather chair, smoking a pipe, and tell me stories. It was very comforting. I still remember the smell of his cherry tobacco.

When he died, everyone was in shock. Then his widow, Peg, suffered a heart attack a few days later and ended up in the hospital. Because of this, my grandfather's dog, a terrier named Johann, was left on his own with no one to take care of him. The dog was my grandfather's constant companion. My parents thought it would be best to keep the dog at our place for a few days. Our family lived in an apartment complex that didn't allow pets, so we secretly kept Johann. The dog was so distraught! I could feel how upset he was. He couldn't sleep and cried and threw up all night long. I felt helpless and didn't know what to do. I decided to sit with Johann during the night when everyone was asleep and try to keep him calm. After a few days, he settled down and was able to go stay with other relatives.

It's cool that this dog's spirit came through and remembered me and that I helped him through the nights right after my grandfather died. I was surprised an animal could communicate after death. I never imagined this was possible. To me, this was absolute proof that it was my grandfather Sylvon coming through in the practice session.

Sylvon grew up on a farm in the rural town of Spooner, Wisconsin. His parents Ernest and Nellie were farmers. During the Depression, he dropped out of school in eighth grade and went to work to help support his family. Despite his lack of formal education, he made a career as a self-taught tile contractor.

I know very little about Sylvon's parents. During the Depression they moved to Madison, Wisconsin, a much bigger city, to look for work. Years later, they moved to another farm in Rib Lake, Wisconsin, where Ernest died. I found some old newspaper clippings[1] that list Ernest as being in the hospital for 22 days the year before he died. It's odd that this information is in a local newspaper. It stated the day he was admitted and the date he was discharged, but it didn't mention why he was in the hospital. His obituary didn't mention how he died either, just that he died at home.

I also found that when Ernest lived in Madison, he became a member of the Eagles Club. I wasn't sure what that was, so I looked it up. In 1898, six theater owners founded the Fraternal Order of Eagles in Seattle, Washington. The F.O.E became an organization of humanitarians similar to the Freemasons. They performed rituals and had secret rites and passwords. As a side note I found it interesting that until the late 1970s, to be admitted into the Eagles you had to be a white person. Thankfully, things have changed. I think the family struggled financially to keep the farm, so perhaps joining a group like this helped Ernest feel a kinship with others going through the same thing. This was all I was able to find on Ernest and Nellie. No living relative has any memories to share, so I decided to go back to the distant past to research the origins of the Blair family.

---

[1] *The Marshfield News-Herald*, (1948)

Psychic Ancestry

I traced the Blair family back to the 16th century in Edinburgh, Scotland. Many of the Blairs lost their estates and wealth in the Jacobite uprisings in and around Scotland that began in the late 1600s. Subsequently, some parts of the family moved to Ulster, Ireland, and were considered Scots-Irish. The first Blair to arrive in the United States was my 7th great-grandfather, John Blair, in 1718. In search of opportunity, many people who lived in Northern Ireland immigrated to New England in pursuit of land ownership and religious freedom. John was one of them. He sailed in a group of five ships, on the Elizabeth. The ships landed in Boston, and John settled in Cumberland County, Pennsylvania.

In Pennsylvania, John Blair was a local pastor and owned several hundred acres of land. His land was called a "plantation," which simply meant he owned enough acreage to be designated as such. It was not a plantation as we think of them in Southern states, such as Louisiana's large antebellum homes. Instead, it was a working farmstead, more humble in nature. As my research went along, I came across the will of John Blair. In the will, John leaves his "three Negro slaves," a man, a woman, and their child[2] to his family members, to be sold upon John's death. What? Enslaved people? This stopped me in my tracks. I wasn't surprised this could happen, but it made my heart sink to find this out. I realize many people doing ancestry research come across enslavers in their family trees. I wonder how they deal with this news.

Another Blair named William, perhaps John's grandson, who lived on the same land as John, was an enslaver. I found slave registry records for Cumberland County that listed William's enslaved people, a man and woman, as Vine and Phillip. Both Vine and Phillip escaped at some point. Philip was found and returned to

---

[2] *The use of the words Negro and slave are used to show a historical context, along with being taken from a will and legal documents, and are not advocated by the author.*

William, and Vine a few years later. Once returned, they were listed as "slaves for life" on the paperwork. Finding out this history and their names was, to say the least, incredibly unsettling.

Today, it's hard not to judge my ancestors for their choices. It's also a judgment on the history of our country. My ancestors came to America to flee a restrictive life in Ireland, yet they enslaved others and took away their freedom. The Blair motto "I love the virtuous" doesn't apply here. The Blairs of the 12th century likely intended for their descendants to take the moral high ground, which is not how history, or I, view the case of John and William Blair.

I was initially conflicted about adding this story to my history of the Blairs. Even though slavery was outlawed in America a long time ago, the effects are still pervasive today. People of color continue to be oppressed by our society.

When I was in high school, I was out walking with one of Black friends. He needed to use the bathroom. Luckily, we were near my house, so we stopped by, but my dad wouldn't let him come in because of his race. We lived in a diverse neighborhood with a mix of White and Black people, so I was baffled by this. I guess it never dawned on me that my dad would react that way because my friend was Black. I was so embarrassed and ashamed of his behavior. I didn't know what to do. We continued walking and found a store to stop into to use their restroom. Writing about my family's role in racial prejudice and enslavement is helping me come to terms with this and start the healing process.

I was relieved to discover that, 55 years after John Blair's death, other Blair ancestors would take a stand against enslavers. Thomas and David Blair, John Blair's great-grandsons, were brothers and pioneers who lived in Pike County, Illinois. In 1824, they traveled together from their home to Atlas, Illinois, a round trip of about 150 miles by canoe and by foot, to vote against the legalization of slavery in Illinois. Years later, they both became members of the

State Legislature. Finding this fact made me feel slightly better, but it didn't erase the pain of my ancestor's actions.

I was hopeful that I could contact John Blair, my ancestor, and surely he would show remorse for his actions. I spent some time trying to connect with him in a mediumship session. He did come through. I saw him standing in a field, wearing clothing that looked to be from the colonial era, including a wig on his head. Weird, I thought, that he would be standing in a field, wearing a wig. Normally, this would be worn in town or on a formal occasion, as a sign that a person had money and substance. Psychic images are often symbolic, so I took it as such. John also showed me some farm tools and let me know his family worked hard on his land. He said telepathically, "Owning slaves was important to show my status in life." He did not apologize. This is not the response I expected. It was very disappointing. I'm hoping I glimpsed a moment of his life during the time he lived and not how his soul went on to evolve in the afterlife.

I believe that once we pass on, we review our lives, and continue to learn and grow on the other side. Through mediumship, spirits have communicated to me their goals and projects they're working on. Some are pretty busy. We are all given choices, whether we exist on the material plane or in the spirit world. When you pass on, I think you can choose to do nothing or to work on yourself and continue to grow spiritually. It may be, I tapped into who John Blair "was" at that time in history.

John Blair's son, Alexander Blair, was a pioneer who settled in Bourbon County, Kentucky. This was the frontier. To the settlers, it was a land of mystery, wonder and danger. In the late 1700s, Alexander founded a settlement called Blair's Station to protect his family, friends, and neighbors from indigenous attacks. Fights between the indigenous peoples and settlers happened regularly. And it's not surprising there was fighting and killing. People were trying to drive the tribes from their ancestral lands. The Blair family had been in the New World since the early 1700s, so they no doubt played their part in this. So far, it was hard to find any fondness for my Blair ancestors who came first to America. I wanted to admire them and feel appreciation for the spirit they showed to start their lives over, but I wasn't feeling it.

My colonial and early American ancestors were part of the violent struggle for power and control over which peoples would become the rulers of North America. In researching my ancestors, I didn't realize I would be writing about enslavement and oppression. Knowing the role my ancestors played in this helps me to tell the true story of what happened.

Further down the ancestry line, I came across a Mary Blair who is my 3rd great-grandmother. At the age of 16, she married her first cousin, Theodore Blair. They were married for 46 years, until his death. Theodore Blair was one of three male Blairs who married their first cousins. What's up with that? I discovered it was common at this time in history, but it made me feel uncomfortable to find this out. Mary had 13 children. Only six of them survived infancy. I can't imagine what a trauma that must have been for her. I was curious if marrying a first cousin had anything to do with the children's health. I checked into this. Apparently, most babies born to cousin couples are healthy, although there is a higher risk of an inherited condition.

I wondered where the seven children who died were buried. Were they all together in the same cemetery? I searched every graveyard in the counties they lived in for the Blair kids, but no luck. If they lived on farmland, it's possible they could be buried in a family cemetery on their property, but it would be hard to find any record of this.

I tried several times to contact Mary Blair in mediumship sessions, hoping she would share where her seven children were buried. She did come through, but only to show me she was reunited with all her children in the afterlife. It was great to see them all together as a group in my mind's eye.

Mary Blair's husband Theodore Blair was a carpenter and worked in the lead mines in Wisconsin. He also fought in the Civil War. He was stationed in Nashville, Tennessee, and in the early part of 1865, he was wounded or became ill and was taken out of duty. This information is from a newspaper clipping from a Nashville paper[3]. The article also describes the weather in the area at the time: *"The weather is this section is beautifully mixed. Rain, hail, snow, wind, calm, heat and cold, storm and sunshine-succeed each other with the most regular irregularity imaginable."* This is funny to me, because it perfectly describes the weather in Wisconsin where I grew up.

One of Mary's surviving daughters, Fannie and I, share the same birthday. Fannie was born on October 23rd, 1857, exactly 100 years before me. Her husband deserted her and her young son after only three years of marriage. She divorced him and went on to have two more marriages.

It's interesting to me how my ancestors struggled financially after coming to America. Some were prosperous initially, but as time went on and for various reasons, many lost their fortunes. Some became farmers in the Midwest and could barely eke out a living. As I mentioned before, my grandfather Sylvon dropped out of school at an early age and went into the workforce.

So what is the essence of the Blair family today? Are they more in line with the clan motto? I would say, yes, based on the Blairs I know.

We're going to leave the Scottish clans now and travel to the midwestern United States and meet my mysterious ancestor, William Santas.

---

[3] *The Nashville Daily Press and Times*, (1865)

Part Three
Spook Hill: Wonewoc Spiritualist Camp & William Santas

Photo credit: Dreamstime.com

Family Tree for William Santas
My 3rd great-grandfather
Note: This is not a complete family tree

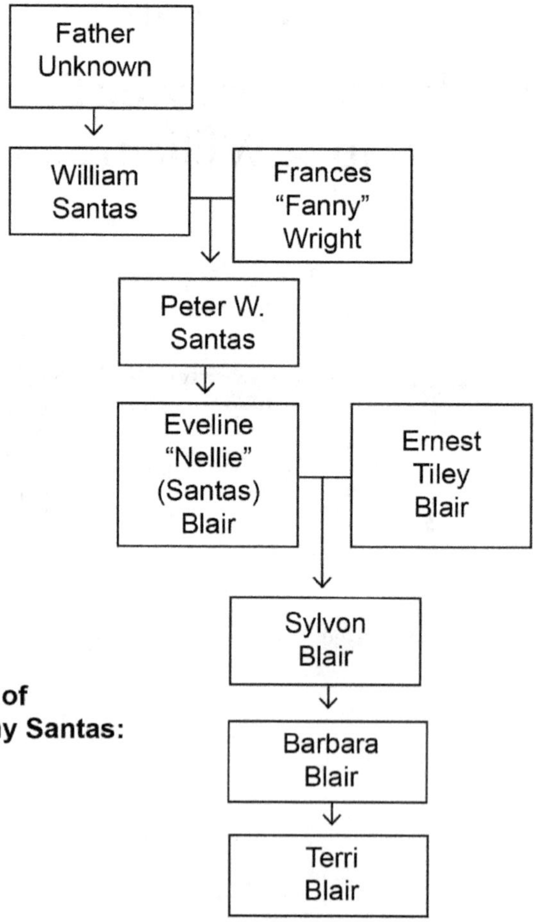

```
Father Unknown
    ↓
William Santas —— Frances "Fanny" Wright
            ↓
        Peter W. Santas
            ↓
    Eveline "Nellie" (Santas) Blair —— Ernest Tiley Blair
                        ↓
                   Sylvon Blair
                        ↓
                  Barbara Blair
                        ↓
                   Terri Blair
```

Other children of William & Fanny Santas:
Hiram
Harve
William
Levi
George

Chapter 11
Spook Hill: William Santas

On a warm summer day, I was with several women in the main lodge at Wonewoc Spiritualist Camp for a psychic development class. Dry weather had been forecasted for the day with no rain in sight. Suddenly, as class began, the sky started to darken, and it began to look like nighttime. The wind kicked up as lightning lit the sky and thunder began to roll. The rain came down in torrents. The bathrooms were in another building, so I ran out into the crazy storm. There was no path, only grass. I didn't plan for rain; I wore sandals on my feet. As I ran through the puddles and soaked grass all I could think of was worms getting stuck between my toes. The rain kept up like this for two solid hours for the entirety of the class. My thought was that my ancestor William Santas was up to his tricks.

A year before this rainy day, ancestry detective work led me to discover Wonewoc Spiritualist Camp. I was researching my ancestors, one of them being my 3rd great-grandfather, William Santas. There was a mystery surrounding verification who his father was, so I traveled to the small town of Wonewoc, Wisconsin to see what I could uncover.

The spiritualist camp sits high up on a wooded hill in central Wisconsin, at the eastern edge of the Driftless Area. It began sometime in the 1850s and was originally called Unity Park. Here psychics and mediums gave their readings in big white tents that were set among the tall pines on the bluff. There is an old craggy stone staircase in the town that leads up to the camp. In 1874 the camp as it's known today was founded by spiritualists from Lily Dale, New York, one of the original spiritualist camps in the United States. Quaint cabins replaced the tents and are set in a circle around a main chapel. All the cabins are numbered and uniquely decorated for use by the mediums who give readings.

In 1874 an independent railroad line began service from Chicago to Winona, Minnesota, with a stop in Wonewoc. People could attend the camp, stay, and rent a tent at the base of the hill, for three dollars a week. I imagine the women of the day with their long skirts struggling up the bluff, their hats catching on tree branches as they climbed the stone staircase. They would have made the trip to have a reading or attend a spirit circle, otherwise known as a séance. Here spirits were said to tap out messages from beyond. The number of taps represented a letter of the alphabet to form a message. Later, in the 1940s and 1950s, up to 600 people per day visited the camp.

In the mid 1800s, spiritualists churches and camps were popping up everywhere across the United States, due to the popularity of the Fox Sisters. Spiritualism was all the rage. In 1847, Maggie and Kate Fox lived on a farm in Hydesdale, New York. They reported rappings or knockings in the house, said to be spirits. Soon the curious and skeptical alike traveled in droves to New York to see for themselves. They did regular public demonstrations with spirits tapping out messages. The Spiritualist movement spread from New York, up and down the east coast, and west into Ohio, Wisconsin, and neighboring states. By the 1860s up to 80,000 people in the state of Wisconsin identified as spiritualists.

I had an interest in spiritualism at an early age. When I was twelve years old, my girlfriends and I thought it would be fun to experiment with a séance to summon the spirit of a dead person. My mom had a plaster bust of John F. Kennedy that sat on a table in our living room. It was a weird decorative object. One night we decided we would try to contact the spirit of JFK using the plaster head as our conduit. We lit candles and turned out the lights. We asked his spirit to give us a sign he was there. We waited and waited, but absolutely nothing happened! We were disappointed and a bit relieved. Of course, he may be a busy man even on the other side and didn't appear on demand just because a few kids requested his presence. It was fun to give it a try.

The Santas story begins with my family tree that I was building in Ancestry.com. In the program, as a person builds their tree, the program presents probable parents of each person that is being researched. When I added William Santas, his surname was listed as Santas/Antes for some reason. The program then populated his father as William Antes. I wasn't sure why his father's name was given as Antes, but surely it was correct. I continued to populate the tree and build out the Antes family history. I assumed somewhere along the line William changed his name from Antes to Santas, since people of his era did this sort of thing.

It turns out that the Antes family has quite a history in the United States, first settling in Pennsylvania from Germany in the early 1700s. Family members played a significant role in the Revolutionary War. They were musket and cannon makers and helped our country win battles against the British with their inventions. They even hosted George Washington at one of their homes in Pennsylvania. Some of the family moved to Wisconsin in the mid-1800s with the lure of inexpensive farmland.

I spent over a year collecting data on the Antes family and was proud that my ancestors played such an important role in American history. However, something kept bugging me. Intuitively I felt something wasn't quite right about this information. I couldn't find out much about William Santas because of the change in surname from Antes to Santas. I needed to find the reason he changed his name to prove who he was. I contacted several people on Ancestry.com who also had William Santas/Antes in their family trees, but no one knew anything about him or why his name would have both surnames.

I was frustrated. I kept hitting roadblocks in finding out about him. I did discover that he lived in New York State before moving to Wisconsin in the mid 1850s, but there were many years of missing information before this and during the time he lived in Wisconsin.

I decided I would try to contact him via mediumship to see if he could fill in some blanks. I tried several times but not all the dead cooperate! Many times, when I tried to search for him on genealogy sites, my computer would suddenly freeze up or crash. When typing up notes about him, the dreaded spinning wheel would show up and I would lose the file I was working on. This happened so often, it almost seemed like he was sabotaging my progress. Why would William block my research?

One day, I decided to give it one more try. I sat in a comfy chair in front of my fireplace and tried to contact him. He came through just barely. I saw the image of an older man, smoking a pipe. He didn't convey much, but he did show me a pocket watch with a sailing schooner engraved on the back. I didn't see how this schooner would relate to him, since the Antes family had been in the United States since the late 1700s, and he was most likely born here, although I couldn't find his birth record.

I was able to locate his grave marker on Findagrave.com, so I knew he was buried in Hillsboro, which is near Wonewoc, Wisconsin. My partner Joe and I decided to make a trip from Milwaukee to Hillsboro to check out William's grave in person. We planned that we would visit the cemetery and then I would spend the afternoon at the local historical society to do family research.

Once in Hillsboro, we pulled over to the side of the road to check the navigation to help us find the gravesite. As we did this,

I happened to notice a long winding road on the navigation screen called "Santas Loop." We made a note and thought we would look for it later. Maybe it was a connection. Or maybe it was a seasonal Christmas attraction. Santa's Loop.

We located the cemetery and found the grave almost immediately. It was interesting because across from William's headstone was a cannon. I thought, "A clue!" The Antes family were cannon makers. We had some time before my meeting at the historical society, so we went to look for Santas Loop.

We found the loop road, which was a lovely hilly drive through farmland dotted with homes and farms. And guess what? On one property sat another cannon! We were on to something. Later, at the historical society, a volunteer named Iris, a retired schoolteacher and lifelong resident of the area, was able to confirm that Santas family members were the original owners of much of the land on Santas Loop. Some of the family still lives there today. I was able to copy names, addresses and phone numbers from the local phone directories of the current Santas residents on Santas Loop. I intended to contact them to see if they could shed some light on the Santas/Antes name mystery.

After I'd been with Iris for a few hours doing research, I started to pack up to leave. As I walked to the door, she turned to me and said, "Did you know there is a spiritualist camp in Wonewoc?" I was surprised. Somehow, she knew I would be open to this information. Not everyone is interested in spiritualism. I was excited to hear about the camp and couldn't wait to check it out.

Wonewoc, a small town of just over 800 people about 15 miles from Hillsboro, has an interesting history. In a valley surrounded by bluffs, sounds echo over a great distance. The indigenous people called the town "howling hills" or "they howl." They attributed this to animals or the spirits that inhabited the region. During the middle to late 1800s, the town was home to three churches and four fraternal organizations, including Freemasons and the Independent Order of Odd Fellows, and the Wonewoc Spiritualist Camp.

The town is tucked against the bottom of a long, high hill, squeezed in between the hill and the Baraboo River. The layout is long and skinny with trees and the bluff blocking the sunlight. I imagine that back before cars, the town had many muddy streets. It's not a sunny place. Many of the buildings are placed against the side of the hill as though they're trying to hide.

A few weeks after our initial visit to the area and the Historical Society, Joe and I headed back to Wonewoc, where I would attend the spiritualist camp for the first time. I planned to spend the day taking a class and getting a reading from one of the resident mediums.

On the appointed day, we arrived at the camp, and I walked down the path to the designated cabin to have my reading. I settled into a chair across from the woman who was the medium. Candles were burning and crystals were placed on the table in front of me. It was very cozy and welcoming. I felt calm and relaxed, plus excited to see what she would tell me. When she began the reading, she didn't ask me anything about myself, she just started talking.

Messages came through from several of my relatives, including my mom, my grandfather, an aunt, and others. This was so interesting! During the reading, all the messages were verified by facts only I would know about these family members. At the end of our session, she asked me if I had anyone else I wanted to hear from. I told her I had an ancestor I was researching named William and asked if he had any messages for me. He did. He told her the townspeople used to call the spiritualist camp "Spook Hill," and that church people never went up there. Then he said something surprising. He said I should *stop* looking for information about him and take a break for a while. Then our session ended. I had no idea why he would want me to stop. Maybe he was getting annoyed at my poking into his past. In any case, it made sense to give it break since I was getting nowhere with my research about him.

I took a break for several months but couldn't stand the unsolved mystery! I had the addresses of a few people who still lived on Santas Loop, so I selected one of the Santas family members and sent him a letter. The letter detailed my research to date and that I was hoping to learn more about my ancestor William Santas. Several days later I received a call from the man I sent the letter to. And he told me he was a descendent of William Santas. It looked like we were distant cousins.

On our next trip to Wonewoc, Joe and I met with him, and he presented us with a family document hand-written by his great-grandfather, when he was in his 80s. In the document, he talks about William immigrating to the United States in the mid 1800s from Spain! Not Germany. His last name was Santas not Antes. He was one of nine sons, eight of whom were trained to be priests. One of his brothers also immigrated to Wisconsin and ran a church out of his home on Santas Loop. Also revealed in the family history is the fact that William was a sailor at one time and made his living working on ships! Is this why he showed me the pocket watch with the schooner engraved on it? And, is this why he wanted me to stop my research? Did he know I was barking up the wrong family tree?

After this revelation, I went back to Ancestry.com and other genealogy sites to see if I could find any records of the arrival of William Santas in the United States. There was nothing. Then it dawned on me that if he was coming from Spain, his first name would be Guillermo, the Spanish name for William. I was able to find one record of a G. Santas coming to the States from Spain in 1834. He was born in 1801, so this timing could make sense. I also contacted two local historical societies in New York State where census records showed he had lived, but they came up with nothing. He remained elusive. To date, I have not been able to find who his parents were, but the search continues.

I now knew that William Santas was not from the Antes family nor related in any way. It was simply a coincidence that there was a cannon near his gravestone. I also found out the other cannon on Santas Loop was put there by the current property owner and has no apparent connection to the Antes history.

My online research led me down the wrong path. I have no idea how the William Antes name got in there with William Santas, but it is not correct. I later learned that sometimes information may be added to a family tree in online databases, that comes from family lore without real documentation to back it up. Therefore, I now take extra time to verify the information that is presented to me in this program with other sources.

I feel that William led me to discover a history and ancestors I didn't know I had in Western Wisconsin. My research about him also led me to Spook Hill, the place of the abrupt thunderstorms on that late summer day. Was it William's energy sending the rain and crashing my computer? In my family whenever there is a funeral, almost without fail there is a thunderstorm or snowstorm at the burial. I like to think the spirits are making their presence known.

Santas Loop Rd. in Wonewoc, WI.

Chapter 12
Wonewoc Mediumship Class

In researching my ancestry, I've had success using mediumship to contact specific people and ancestors who have passed on. Earlier I gave an example of this, such as my 2nd great-grandmother Eliza telling me about "Jimmy." I wondered, how far should I take this? Do I want to learn more about mediumship? Could I help people by bringing forth messages from their loved ones?

In August of 2023, Wonewoc Spiritualist Camp was holding a three-day mediumship training class. If I decided to attend, I would be immersed in an intense learning session. I hesitated for all of three minutes after finding out about the class and signed up. This class would teach me how to give readings for other people without knowing who would come through in advance. This is not something I had tried before. It made me nervous to consider. I was hoping I would be able to do this. I didn't want to fail, and I was excited to learn more.

One may ask, what is the difference between mediumship and other psychic skills? Psychic information comes to me clairvoyantly, in the form of images or telepathic conversation that conveys a message. The source of this is often difficult to identify. With extrasensory perception, I can tap into information that is hidden to the normal senses.

In mediumship, a spirit of a deceased person gives me information directly. Some mediums can see dead people as if they are real, although that hasn't happened for me. I see them in my mind's eye and feel their presence. In a mediumship reading, the spirit or spirits give a message for the person for whom the session is being conducted, provide clues to who they are, and sometimes manifest their presence in smells or sounds. For instance, one's grandmother might show up in a reading, provide evidence as to who she is, and give a message. There may be the smell of her perfume in the air as a physical manifestation.

When August arrived, Joe and I packed up the car and headed west out of Milwaukee for Wonewoc. After a few hours' drive, we arrived at our hotel in Mauston, Wisconsin, where we would stay for the long weekend.

The class was to start the next day. I had some time when we arrived, so we went to the Juneau County Court House to do some more ancestry research. The beautiful Art Deco courthouse was built in 1939. It was quiet inside, with long shadowy hallways and echoes of footsteps and hushed conversations, with the warm wind blowing through when the doors were opened.

I wanted to research exactly where my ancestor William Santas first settled in the area. His children owned land on Santas Loop, but I didn't find that William did. At the courthouse, a clerk told me the old land records were kept in the basement. I followed him down the hall to a room where a spiral staircase descended to the lower level. I slowly made my way down the metal steps to a narrow room. It was dimly lit and was lined with old bookcases. I was directed to the books from the 1870s when William lived in the area. And then the clerk left me alone. I tried not to dwell on my alone status and grabbed a book to begin my search for William's property.

I opened the book and began looking through the handwritten list of names. I stood close to the stairwell as it had the best light for reading. As I scrolled down the page, I had the distinct feeling someone was standing behind me, even though I was alone.

Ignoring this, I kept reading the names in the book. Then, there it was! William Santas was listed along with the location of his land. In 1870, he purchased 26 acres on Sosinsky Road, which today is next to Santas Loop.

I closed the book and made my way back upstairs to report my findings to the clerk. He pulled up a plat map on his computer to show me where the Santas property originally was. The map showed the site to be on a hill where the road makes a distinct curve, with buildings on both sides. Joe and I decided to take a drive down Sosinsky Road to check it out.

We found the spot and stopped to look. There was a sweeping view of the valley and some barns and sheds that looked quite old, along with a modern house. There were several stone foundations from previous structures that predated the others. We took a minute to stop and admire the landscape. It was then Joe noticed the smell of pipe tobacco. It took me a minute, but then I began to smell it too. There was no one around, at least that we could see. In a previous mediumship session, William showed me that he smoked a pipe. Was it him? I was hoping it was. I felt he was happy we finally found his land. He was the original Santas who brought the family name to Wisconsin.

The next morning, we drove over to the town of Wonewoc for class. Joe planned on dropping me off and then he would head out to explore the area. As we made our way up the hill on the twisty road to the Wonewoc Spiritualist Camp, I was filled with anticipation about what the next few days would bring. The entrance to the camp is marked by a sign and two brick pillars on either side of the driveway. Upon arriving at the now familiar camp, I felt as though I was transported back in time. The weathered cabins set in a circle, the tall pine trees, gravel paths, firepit and funky gift shop all add to the vibe of a proud and enduring history. The parking lot was full, which made me wonder who I would meet.

The instructor was Richard Schoeller, a man with impressive credentials. He's been a medium, lecturer and teacher for over 25 years. He is both funny and charismatic, and asked us to work hard to enhance our skills. Richard told many interesting stories. At age 33, seemingly out of the blue, both sets of his deceased grandparents stood before him. He could see them clearly. This came as quite a shock to him. Two days after that, in his career as a funeral director, he saw the spirit of a woman he was about to bury. She gave him a message to share with her family. This helped him in two ways. The first was learning to trust the information he was receiving from the spirit realm. The second was he immediately learned to shut down or control his newfound ability while working, or out in the public world. His life would never be the same again. He realized his grandparents had appeared to encourage him to recognize his unique spiritual abilities. He began studying mediumship and went on to become a full time medium.

Our class of 14 was a diverse group of various ages. There were mostly women and two men. Some were retired, others were therapists, photographers, holistic practitioners and working mediums. Richard was to teach us a system and practice techniques. Over the course of the class, people would pair up and give readings for each other. For some, this would be the first time doing this.

At the beginning of the class, Richard led us through a series of exercises to loosen us up and help us get to know each other. Everyone was willing to learn, even those who were already mediums. He told us many fascinating stories about mediumship readings he'd done for others during his career. He also kept us laughing with his wit and great sense of humor.

When it was time to give readings with a partner, I momentarily panicked. Could I do this? Okay, I thought, take a deep breath, and give it a shot.

For the first session, I was paired with a friendly man named Jim who would give me a reading. I was relieved I didn't have to go first. We sat in chairs facing one another. Per Richard's instruction, Jim asked me if he could read for me. I answered, "Yes." It's vital to ask permission so both reader and "sitter" are in alignment.

Jim gave me this reading:

"I have an older man here. He is telling me you are his favorite. You are the only one paying attention. He's saying that you and he are connected by DNA, and he is your ancestor. He's wearing a red plaid shirt and bib overalls. He's showing me canning jars full of fruit and vegetables. He is also showing me the land he lived on. It's hilly and there is water nearby. He knows you are writing about ancestors and supports you in this. He is showing me a connection between the two of you by a silvery thread of light."

That was enough evidence for me. I immediately knew this was William Santas, my 3rd great-grandfather. Jim didn't learn his name, but I intuitively knew who it was. Part of learning mediumship is to trust my gut feelings, which I did in this case. William showing himself in bib overalls with canning jars is symbolic of being a farmer, which he was. The property he owned is hilly and there are small streams nearby.

The part about me being his favorite is funny. I feel all the computer crashes that happen when I research him is his way of teasing me. You only tease people you like, right?

After this reading, I was excited about the outcome, but didn't have time to process the information, as it was time to switch readers. It was now my turn to give Jim his reading.

I asked Jim, "May I read for you?" He answered yes, affirming the connection between us. I was used to closing my eyes to give a reading. It's easier for me to concentrate that way, but Richard was teaching us to read with our eyes open. This is more difficult, but is engaging to the person you are sitting across from. It's more personal. It was uncomfortable to look directly at Jim, since he sat inches away from me, so I looked slightly away and to the side of him instead. Then I felt a light tapping on my right shoulder, as if someone was poking me with their finger. I began the reading for Jim:

"I see a woman about the same age as you." I could feel her near me. *"She has dark wavy hair about shoulder length. She looks young, but I feel she is in her late 40s. She's wearing a button-down casual blouse."* I felt strongly this woman was Jim's wife or partner, but didn't say it. I didn't feel confident enough to express this at the time, since I was still learning.

I continued: *"She is saying she's okay and is doing well. She's proud of you and the life you're pursuing and says the two of you are still very connected. This woman is telling me she is busy with projects. She is holding up a giant red heart in front of her. I also see a big wooden mixing spoon. She's showing me that she is driving a sporty new car in the afterlife."* Then she started to fade away, so I ended the reading.

During the reading Jim nodded a few times, so I thought I must have received some correct information. Then it was time for us to give each other feedback on the readings we did for one another. Jim told me the woman that came through to me was his wife, Luann. Her physical description matched what I was seeing. She battled breast cancer for seven years and recently passed from the disease. Jim and his wife were very much in tune and worked on their psychic skills together. She was born on Valentine's Day, thus the heart she showed me. She was also a phenomenal baker, so the wooden mixing spoon was a symbol for this. He also confirmed Luann was only a couple years younger than him, so close in age. He mentioned he sometimes feels like she is poking or tapping him at night, like the light tap I had on my shoulder. The car didn't resonate, but maybe she's having a good time driving it on the other side.

Jim connected with William Santas for me, and I was able to connect with Jim's wife. In the moment, I didn't absorb how big this was for both of us. Later that day, it hit me that this was a deeply personal and rewarding experience. I was happy that an ancestor came through another person for me. And not just any ancestor. William Santas, whom I was researching at the time.

We took a break for lunch and came back to do more readings for each other. For the next reading, I was paired with Renee, a pretty lady who is an experienced medium. I read for her first. I was a little intimidated, since she has much experience, but took a breath and started. I was able to connect with her mother, but it was a roundabout way of doing this.

With my eyes open, sitting facing Renee, I saw a man in my mind's eye: *"I see a tall, nerdy, balding man with glasses."* Renee couldn't think of anyone she knew who matched that description. I thought, okay, I will push him aside, but the man wasn't going away. *"He's not moving. He's saying, I'm an oncology doctor. Does this make sense to you?"* Renee nodded. I then noticed Renee's mother standing off to the side of the doctor. The man was there to coax her mother to come through. *"Your mom is saying, do we really have to do this? It was so long ago."* I now knew that her mom died of cancer, but I wanted to know what type of cancer. *"I'm going to see if I can sense where the cancer was. I get the feeling it was in her chest, but wait, now it feels like it's in her abdomen. Your mom was very graceful even in the dying process. Everyone loved her. She is conveying her love and support for you."*

After the reading, Renee confirmed her mother died of colon cancer, which eventually spread to other parts of her body. She was a very beloved and graceful woman. She died over 40 years ago, so it made sense that her mom thought of this as old news. This

Psychic Ancestry

reading brought up emotions for Renee, as she teared up. She felt a real connection to her mother during the session.

Now it was Renee's turn to read for me. "*I have a man here. He is your father. He's showing me pain in his shoulder and back and is having a hard time breathing. You were not in the room when he died and had a problematic and distant relationship. Your dad says he is proud of you.*"

This reading was accurate. My relationship with my dad was troubled, going back to early childhood. He died of lung cancer in his mid-seventies. He was misdiagnosed for years and always thought he had heart issues. He did suffer from shoulder and arm pain, as well as back pain. It turned out this was all a part of his disease. When he was finally correctly diagnosed, he had stage four cancer. In the reading, he mentioned he was proud of me, which he never conveyed to me when he was alive. It's true, I was not there when he died.

During the sessions in the class, other spirits came through in readings for me, including my uncle Dick and my maternal grandmother. Uncle Dick was my dad's younger brother. Jill, the woman giving me the reading described him perfectly: *He said to her, "We're the blonds in the family." He's tall and wearing a suit.*" The blond comment meant he and I are both blond, which is unusual on my father's side of the family. I also have a photograph of him in a suit as she described.

This three-day class was rewarding. The entire group bonded, yet felt exhausted and a bit spaced-out by the end of it. Grounding was needed. Richard explained, "We must expand our awareness as the people who are in the spiritual realm meet us, in the focusing of their awareness on us in the physical realm." This is how we connect to spirit. This can be tiring for mere mortals. It was an incredible experience. I felt as though I got to know everyone in the class well since I was meeting so many of their departed relatives!

As Joe and I were heading out of town to drive back to Milwaukee, we drove to William's property for one last look. As we slowed at the crest of the hill on the curve, we rolled down the windows to smell the pipe tobacco.

Entrance to Wonewoc Spiritualist Camp, 2023.

Part Four

My Polish Ancestors

Photo credit: Warsaw-Dreamstime.com

Family Tree for the Skis (Niedzialkowski)
Note: This is not a complete family tree

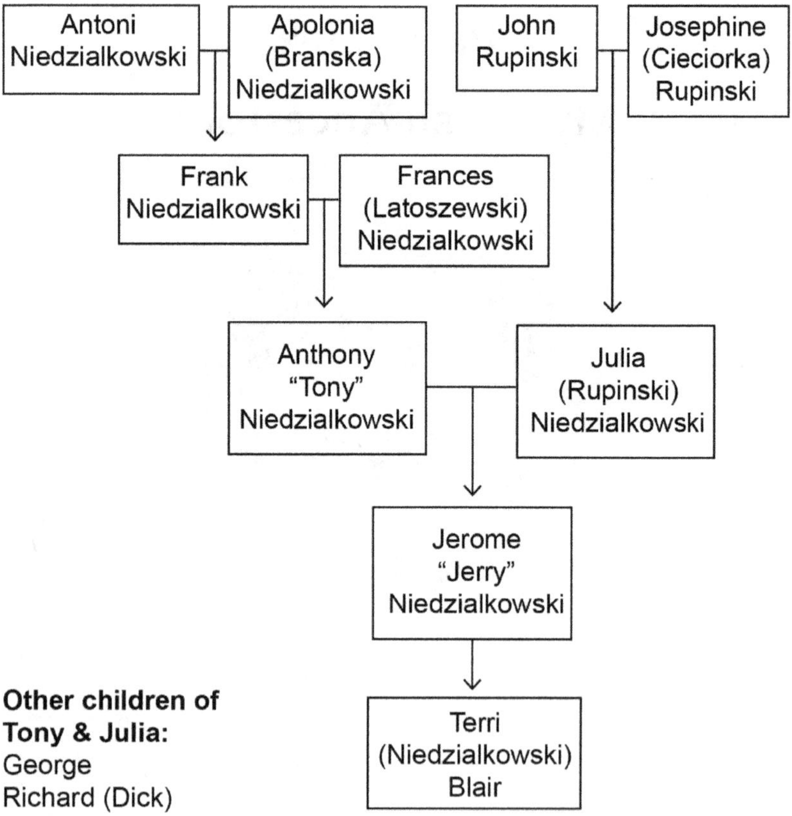

- Antoni Niedzialkowski — Apolonia (Branska) Niedzialkowski
- John Rupinski — Josephine (Cieciorka) Rupinski
- Frank Niedzialkowski — Frances (Latoszewski) Niedzialkowski
- Anthony "Tony" Niedzialkowski — Julia (Rupinski) Niedzialkowski
- Jerome "Jerry" Niedzialkowski
- Terri (Niedzialkowski) Blair

Other children of Tony & Julia:
George
Richard (Dick)
Diane (Dolly)
Susie
Joyce
Margie

Chapter 13
The Skis as Ancestors

Niedzialkowski. This is the Polish surname I was born with. Fourteen letters. Life was not easy with this name. School teachers couldn't pronounce it, nor did it fit into the allotted squares on paper forms. I first noticed there was something different about me when I wrote my name on the chalkboard at school. All the other children's names were much shorter. Mine kept going.

When I began researching my past, I didn't want to write about my Polish ancestors. Not because I'm not interested in them, but because of my difficult relationship with my father. The thought of it made me cringe.

To outsiders it looked as though my dad and I got along well. Especially because of the annual summertime trips with him and my Uncle George to the Edgar Cayce Institute in Virginia Beach. But during the car ride from Milwaukee, my dad and I would often bicker the entire time. He would pick fights. I'm a peace lover, not a fighter, but I believe in self-preservation. So I defended myself.

My dad was an active alcoholic for my growing up years. He was also a hard worker. He held a full-time job, plus took on side projects during evenings and on weekends. Despite this, our family struggled financially. He could be funny and charming, yet cruel and verbally abusive. My dad was highly critical of me. It seemed I didn't do anything right in his eyes. We never got along. We still don't. He comes around in spirit with a strong smell of cigarette smoke. He was a heavy smoker. I ask him to go away and come back with a good smell. To date, he has not.

I only bring up my dad here, because he is the reason I had little interest in exploring the Polish side of my family. However, I feel as though his brother, my uncle George, is prompting me from the other side to explore my Polish ancestry. He doesn't want our ancestors to be ignored. George has come through to me several times since he died, usually during readings with mediums. Through them, he gives me messages of support and encouragement. It's a treat when he shows up. He died in 2001, from Alzheimer's, at 67 years old. There were a few years of decline before his death, so we weren't close at the end. I miss him and the long talks we had about all kinds of topics, including parallel universes, black holes, and life after death.

On one of our trips in the 1980s, my dad and I traveled with George to Virginia Beach. We were attending a conference and looked forward to meeting up with friends we'd met over the years. On the three-day driving trip from Milwaukee, my dad and I fought as usual. Once we arrived, I felt drained, despite the beautiful surroundings. After checking into The Marshalls motel, I headed to the beach for a walk in the warm sunshine.

George beat me to it; he was already there. From a distance, I noticed his unmistakable silhouette, tall and thin, facing the waves, tossing juggling pins in the air. I quickly walked over to him, wanting sympathy. I complained to him about my dad's treatment of me on the drive out. George said, "Let's take a walk." It was a brilliant day. The white sand was warm on my feet and the blue sky empty of clouds. We strolled alongside the water.

As we walked, George said "You need to cut your dad some slack. He lived through some rough things in his childhood." He explained that my grandfather, Tony, abused my grandmother, Julia, by beating her and verbally degrading her. This was shocking and unexpected news about my grandparents. Then I wondered why

George would want to tell me this. Surely, he knew it was upsetting to me to find out something so awful. I never would have guessed what had gone on behind the scenes in their marriage.

George continued, "Many nights, our parents fought bitterly." George said that when this happened my dad was the one delegated by his siblings to sneak down the stairs from the bedrooms and watch what was happening in the kitchen below. He would then report back to his four sisters and two brothers. Once my dad watched my grandfather dump an entire pot of spaghetti on my grandmother's head because he was angry. Later, I realized that George told me this so I would have compassion for my dad, because he lived with the horror of witnessing his mother being mistreated and abused.

Then George told me another thing I didn't know. My grandfather Tony was not George's real father. Julia was pregnant when she met Tony and he agreed to marry her, knowing this. George had a difficult relationship with Tony, which he felt that he came to terms with after Tony died. Again, I wondered, why did George tell me this? It was more George's story than my dad's, but it showed a bigger picture.

In that time, I had no idea about the real family dynamic during my father's childhood. My grandparents lived in a two-story house in an established Polish neighborhood in West Allis, Wisconsin. As a young kid, I remember my grandfather Tony was typically gruff and grumpy. My grandmother was pretty, with dark wavy hair, and wore rouge and lipstick. As a kid, I loved being at my grandparents' house with my sister, brother, and many cousins, especially George's two sons. It often got a little wild. There was an endless flow of sugary drinks and bowls filled with candy everywhere. We could run around freely, and no one tried to stop us. Pure fun. To us it was the best place to be, even if my grandfather was crabby.

The adults were busy drinking, smoking, and playing card games and were oblivious to what the kids were doing. At times, they would sit around my grandfather's old-time radio on the porch for hours and listen to a baseball game.

They had a lovely yard with cherry, pear, and apple trees. My grandmother was a good cook and made pies with the fruit. However, often when walking into her kitchen the strong smell of sauerkraut assaulted my senses. There was usually a slow cooker filled with it and some sort of simmering meat. I focused on the candy.

Christmas at their house was festive. The decorations were extravagant. There was a huge tree bursting with ornaments and silver tinsel hanging from every branch. A revolving color wheel aimed at the tree. It rotated and flashed red to green to blue every few seconds. It was psychedelic, as we said in the 1960s. There were gifts for all the grandchildren, piled high under the tree.

Many people have close relationships with their grandparents. Even though we visited often, I didn't really know my Polish grandparents very well. I can't remember a time that I had a private conversation with either of them. They were first-generation Americans, children of immigrants who moved to the US. Sometimes they spoke Polish with each other. This made them seem exotic and somewhat distant.

When I was older, my dad told me that when they were kids, my grandfather would take him and his two brothers to the basement and make them box with each other. Tony was an amateur boxer when he was younger and thought his kids should know how to fight. This is telling. It seems like a brutal way to teach kids to box, by encouraging them to punch each other in the face. Learning boxing is about training, jumping rope, sparring with gloves, and hitting a punching bag. Not your brother. Not in the face.

West Allis was a tough and gritty place then. It was a factory town. People worked hard and they liked to drink. Maybe Tony wanted his sons to be able to protect themselves when needed.

As a young man, my dad enlisted in the army and was stationed in Germany. During that time, Tony stole from him. My dad sent money home each month and his dad agreed to save it for him. My parents were engaged at the time, and they needed the cash to start their life together. Once my dad returned from the service, he was stunned to find out his dad spent his earnings and didn't save a penny for him. Tony also sold my dad's car without letting him know and kept the money. Thus, despite his hard work and planning, my dad began his married life without any savings, or a car.

I understand now how my dad's upbringing may have influenced his own behavior later in life. As a child he watched domestic violence taking place, along with having a mean and untrustworthy father. After George's revelation, I did feel sorry for my dad, but it didn't excuse his own actions towards me and others.

With Uncle George psychically urging me on, I began my Polish ancestry research, starting with my dad's parents. It proved to be harder than I thought, since much of the information is presented in the Polish language.

I discovered my grandmother Julia's parents, Josephine, and John Rupinski, emigrated to America from an area near Warsaw, Poland, in 1891. Warsaw at the time was a province of Russia and under the control of Czar Nicholas II. Between 1795-1918, Poland was partitioned by Austria, Prussia, and Russia into three parts. In each of the regions, ethnic Poles experienced religious persecution, economic troubles, famines, land shortages and chronic unemployment. During those years, many emigrated to urban areas in the Midwest to work in entry-level industrial jobs. According to immigration records, some of my ancestors arrived with only a few dollars in their pockets. I'm sure they hoped America would prove more prosperous and accepting.

Josephine and John first arrived in New York and later settled in Scranton, Pennsylvania, where John worked as a coal miner. Coal mining was common in the parts of Poland where he lived previously, although I don't know if he or his family were miners. They had five children, including my grandmother. Sometime between 1910 and 1920, they relocated to Wisconsin.

West Allis had several thriving Polish American neighborhoods where they could speak Polish and share their culture with others. As a kid, I noticed the old Polish grandmothers or "Bushas" in church wearing "babushkas," traditional flowered scarves, on their heads.

John soon took a job at Allis-Chalmers, a local machinery manufacturer. Allis-Chalmers operated major plants in Milwaukee, Chicago, Scranton, and Cincinnati. The company was in business for over 150 years, from 1847-1999, and for a time was Milwaukee's largest employer. My childhood memory of the industrial complex is of big smokestacks spewing black smoke and metal banging noises coming from within. The place scared me.

Allis-Chalmer's West Allis plant employed almost 10,000 workers in the year 1937. During the Second World War that number doubled to 20,000. The 1940 census shows the population of West Allis at around 36,000 people. It is likely that most families had someone employed there. The company was an industrial powerhouse and, like many large American manufacturers in the past century, it could be a difficult and at times hostile place to work. Most workers in the factory were referred to as "unskilled labor" even after decades of employment. There were volatile union strikes there in the 1940s.

A census record reveals that when my grandmother Julia was 21 years old, she worked at Allis-Chalmers in the Coil Taping department, which is where electrical turbines were measured. The year was 1930, during the Depression. Allis-Chalmers had employed women in factory jobs since the turn of the century. I'd known my grandmother Julia as a mother of seven children, and I never knew she had once been employed as a factory worker. It was not considered glamorous, but she earned a living. My grandfather Tony also worked at Allis-Chalmers. I imagine that is where they met. This large and loud factory was only blocks from the Rupinski and Niedzialkowski family homes.

On the other side of my dad's family tree, my grandfather Tony's parents came from Poland in 1905, also from the Warsaw area. His father, Franciszek (Frank) Niedzialkowski, worked at an iron castings company in West Allis. Frank listed his father Antoni as being Russian on his census record. Antoni was from the Russian area of Poland since he was born in the years Russia controlled the towns near Warsaw. But in the way we think about this history today, he was ethnically Polish.

Frank came to the U.S. the same year as his brother Jan (John) Niedzialkowski. I found a newspaper article[1] about Jan. He was killed by a train, along with four small boys he was escorting on a pleasure outing in 1919, at the age of 36. Two of the boys were his sons. They were caught on two tracks with trains coming from both directions. This is such a sad story. Unfortunately, in doing ancestry research, you sometimes find stories that made the news because they tell of tragedy. I was glad to expand the family tree by adding Jan so he and his family would be remembered. I didn't know about them until I read the article.

With further research, I traced the Niedzialkowski family back to the 1600s and 1700s to what was then Prussia and Polish-Lithuania. They were part of the nobility, which allowed them to own land and hold some political rights and power. I was excited to share this information with George's two sons. Then I realized, this wasn't their heritage.

---

[1] *The Capital Times*, Madison, WI (1919)

Psychic Ancestry

I assumed because George shared with me the fact that Tony wasn't his dad, it must be common knowledge in his family. However, I discovered at a family party that George's sons didn't know anything about this. They were surprised by the news. Because I thought they knew, I had never talked about this with them until I started my ancestry research.

After this disclosure, one of George's sons found old photos of our grandparents in his dad's belongings. He noticed that George labeled pictures of my grandmother, "Ma." But pictures of my grandfather were labeled, "Tony," not "Pa."

Marriage records state my grandparents Tony and Julia were married on July 1, 1933. George was born on January 24, 1934. By looking at these dates, clearly Julia was pregnant when she married Tony, by about two months. This could support George's story about Tony not being his real father.

Anytime there is an unsolved family mystery, and I've exhausted traditional sources, like before, I try to get answers by using mediumship. I connected with my grandmother Julia a few times this way. I asked her to provide clues to who George's real father is. She was happy to see me but didn't have anything to share on the subject. At least not yet. Spirits don't give information on demand. They must be willing. I was a little disappointed by this but felt lucky to connect with my grandmother regardless.

Then an odd thing happened. One winter day, during a meditation, in my mind's eye a man was suddenly standing behind me. He showed up uninvited. His hands were on my shoulders, forcefully, almost as though he was trying to hold me in place. He wore a navy overcoat and was tall with broad shoulders. His brimmed hat looked to be of a military style from the 1930s. He looked familiar, somewhat like George did when he was younger. The man showed me some loose-leaf pieces of lined paper. I could see they were handwritten letters. I asked his name, but he didn't offer it. I felt he was George's real father.

A few weeks later, I contacted my grandmother Julia again. She showed up for me along with George. I asked again for any information she could give about George's father. She didn't say anything. Instead, she showed me an oval-shaped decorative glass bowl. In it were several opened envelopes. She said to me telepathically, "Tell him I read his letters." I could sense a connection between her and the male spirit who appeared to me earlier. A feeling of sadness came over me.

My grandfather Tony died of a heart attack in 1975, dancing the polka at a church picnic, beer in hand. This is what he loved to do. I will remember the image of him dying happy, despite the unsettling things I came to know about him.

Chapter 14
Circumstantial Evidence

In the mid 1970s, I was carjacked. Although it wasn't called that at the time. I had just finished a shift at the retail store where I worked and walked to my car in the parking lot. I got into the driver's side, and suddenly a man got in on the passenger side. He ended up with the car. As I watched my pristine, olive green 1970 Dodge Polara drive away without me, I was in shock. This car was given to me by my grandmother Julia Niedzialkowski only a few months before.

The reason I bring this up is not for sympathy. When she gave me the car, it was a rare moment of connection with my grandmother. I never knew why she chose me; maybe because I was her oldest grandchild. In any case, I really appreciated the gesture and vowed to take excellent care of her car. I felt terrible to have lost it, even if it wasn't my fault. As I mentioned, we didn't have much personal interaction when I was growing up, so her gift meant a lot to me. Now, decades later, I was delving into her intimate relationship with the father of George, whomever he is. It felt invasive in a way, but I decided to dig deeper anyway, to see where this would lead. I'm glad I continued the search.

It felt important to try and figure out who George's father was, mainly because of George's two sons, whom I grew up with. I had recently told them that Tony may not be their grandfather, and they were skeptical and curious. There was no reason not to believe what George told me in Virginia Beach, but Doug, George's eldest son, decided to have his DNA tested with 23andMe. He was interested to see if the test would confirm that we were first cousins, sharing the same set of grandparents. If we had a perfect match, it would be game over, George's dad was Tony. I was excited that he was willing to do the test. We would have an answer in a couple of months.

One of the obvious things about ancestry is that everyone who investigates it is curious about their heritage. George's sons wanted to know more about theirs. Plus, there was the added angle of a spirit making his presence known. And he wasn't shy about it. He came across as a strong personality when he appeared to me and put his hands on my shoulders.

This spirit soon made another appearance. At Wonewoc Spiritualist Camp, during a reading with one of the resident mediums, a tall man wearing a military style or captain's hat showed up. This matched the description of the man who appeared to me months earlier. This was interesting. He didn't seem to have a message, but I felt he wanted me to know he was around and watching.

Meanwhile, George's sons and I thought that while we waited for the DNA results, we would gather as much information as we could relating to George and my grandparents. We wanted to see if George left any clues behind. And it would be just like my uncle to give us a project to work on. When we were kids, his sons, my sister, and I would often get together. We didn't play normal kid games when George was around. He always came up with some sort of mind puzzle for us to work on. For example, he may have told us to name 50 words that started with letter B and ended with an E. Or something equally mind numbing for a kid. We loved it! And now, he presented us with another challenge.

By now it was early spring, and a couple of months since Doug sent in his DNA test, so I wondered if he would have results soon.

I was anxiously waiting. In my research, I wasn't finding anything new to support George's story. Although, through census records, I was able to piece together some things about my grandmother Julia.

Julia was 24 years old in 1933, single and living with her parents. She became pregnant in May of that year, assuming her baby was born at full term, as we believe he was.

I was curious about how she may have met George's father. In the early 1930s in West Allis, Wisconsin, I wondered what a single woman in her 20s would do for fun. Prohibition was still in force. Julia was living in a factory town, and probably craved some glamour and excitement after work and on the weekends. In my memory, my grandmother always wore makeup and dresses.

As a working woman, I imagine her free time was valuable. She most likely wanted to socialize and meet new people. In West Allis there was a theater and concert hall not too far from her house. There was also the State Fair in the summer, but that only lasted a week or two. And there was dancing.

A friend told me that her grandmother used to go to ballrooms with her friends in the 1930s to socialize. At times, she would meet men at the dances, especially those who came in on the ships that docked in Milwaukee Harbor. At the time, Milwaukee had several ballrooms, including the Wisconsin Roof Ballroom, Dreamland, The Crystal, and very close to Julia's house, the Modernistic. Big Band was all the rage, and admission was less than a dollar. Sailors from the Great Lakes Training Base looking for romance and dancing made up a big portion of the patrons.[1] It's possible that Julia met George's father at once of these ballrooms. That could explain the military or captain's style hat the spirit shows up in.

Another scenario is that because Julia was pregnant when she married my grandfather Tony, he *was* George's father. If Julia and

---

[1] *Excerpt from Astortheater.org, Wisconsin Roof Ballroom*

Tony were dating and she got pregnant, they would have married when she discovered the pregnancy. This was not uncommon. But it was not the story George shared with me. And I don't think he was making this up.

I don't know how George learned that Tony was not his father or why he believed this. Perhaps his mother told him on her deathbed. As far as I know, his other siblings knew nothing about this. When I contacted my grandmother through mediumship, she has shown me things, like the letters in the oval bowl, but she is not saying anything more. I asked another medium to try and contact her and she received the same reaction. Julia was not talking.

As the months went by, there was still no word from Doug on his DNA results. I was dying to know the outcome! Would he find more relatives he couldn't identify that could be connected to George's real father? The suspense was driving me nuts. I soon discovered that my cousin had not yet taken the test. He is a very busy man, so it was understandable, but this delayed the results for a while longer.

Later that summer, I again made a trip to Wonewoc Camp for a three-day intensive mediumship and psychic development class. We worked on spirit communication, healing techniques and remote viewing. I was in heaven doing this stuff! On the last day of the class, one of the mediums gave me a message from a male spirit. He was tall and showed up wearing a military style hat: "*I am a grandfather figure, but not your paternal grandfather, and there is a mystery surrounding me that needs to be solved.*" This spirit was not going away, he was still interjecting himself. I knew by the description: he was the same male spirit that had been showing up repeatedly.

The spirit of this man may want me to help him find George. There is much we don't know about the afterlife. We may shift to another level of consciousness when we die, but that doesn't mean we become all-knowing or meet people we never knew in life. For instance, when my great-grandmother Annie died, I don't believe she knew about her true parentage. She may be aware of my findings because she is psychically connected to me now and is learning about it after her death. The spirit who seems to be the real father of George may want me to help figure out how to show George and his family the truth. This was proving to be tricky!

As we continued to look for clues, my cousin Doug found many family photos of Julia and Tony (my grandparents). George wrote notes on the back of the photos, telling who was in them. As I mentioned before, if his parents were in the picture, more often than not, Julia was listed as "Ma" and his dad as "Tony." It was an unusual practice to call your parents by their first names in those years, so this may be a clue. In Virginia Beach that day, George told me his dad and he never got along. Tony wasn't a warm fuzzy guy, and they had a strained relationship. This could be because George was not his biological son and he resented him.

Another thing to note is that George's middle name was Richard. Julia also named one of her sons Richard. Where did this name come from? I do not see this name in the family tree on her side or Tony's. George was also tall, like the spirit that showed up for me. No one else in the family was his height. He was also a unique character, unlike anyone else in the family, including his parents. These are interesting things to note.

Then finally, the DNA results were in! On a hot August afternoon, instead of sitting poolside with a refreshing cocktail, my two cousins and I sat in my living room, with papers and old photos strewn everywhere. If we shared the same set of grandparents and were first cousins, the report would show this. Unfortunately, it wasn't that cut and dried. The DNA findings indicated that it was *possible* that Doug was my first cousin, but he could also be a half cousin. First cousins typically share about 12.5% of their

DNA, and the range is 7.3 to 13.8%. Doug and I share 9.2%. Half cousins share 2.0-11.5%. Which means it was inconclusive that we share both grandparents. Another cousin of mine who has the same maternal grandparents as I do, shares 12.5% of DNA with me. The mystery of George's father remained. This was not what I was expecting. I really hoped for something more solid to go on.

Besides listing shared DNA and indicating possible family relationships, 23andMe also shows a list of countries that one's ancestors came from, going back about 200 years in most cases. Perhaps the countries of Doug's ancestors could provide more clues. His profile included a long list, including the area in Poland that Tony and Julia's grandparents' families came from. But that was only one side of his family tree. I had recently researched George's wife's side of the family to see where they lived in Europe before coming to America. We knew that both of Tony and Julia's families came from the same part of Poland. However, we needed more information on George's wife's side of the family, to see if the list of countries from both Doug's parents are accounted for in his profile.

After comparing the countries, we were left with a few outliers: Belarus, Russia, Ukraine, and Romania. These four countries could not be accounted for with any of Tony, Julia, or George's wife's family members going back to the 1800s. I wondered why my cousin would have DNA from these four countries in his profile. Where did this come from? This could help prove there is another person we don't know of in the family lineup.

Looking at my grandparents together in photos, it always struck me that the two of them didn't seem to go together. My grandmother was pretty, and my grandfather was not. This is not a judgement, it just seemed odd to me as a kid, and later as an adult, that she would have chosen him as a husband. It's another thought to throw into the mix.

Circumstantial Evidence

As of now, we don't have a clear answer. What we have is circumstantial evidence and nothing more. The mysterious spirit in the hat won't let this go, but for now I need to. It's a bit frustrating that the spirit claiming to be George's father can't simply tell me his name. However, I don't always get what I want with spirit communication.

My green Dodge Polara was eventually found. It had been stripped of all tires and usable engine parts. I went to visit it at the dump to say goodbye. The carjacker was never caught, but luckily my grandmother didn't know about this. I decided not to tell her.

The house in West Allis, WI, where my grandparents raised their seven children.

Part Five

Psychic Kin, Protection & Spirit Guides

Chapter 15
In Search of Psychic Kin

There is a theory that psychic abilities are often inherited through the women in a family line, one generation passing it on to the next. Perhaps it's something in the DNA, such as in the case of the Highland Women.

Part of my search for my ancestors began out of a desire to see if I could find more evidence of psychic abilities in my family. This is a difficult task, since there really is no way to know which ancestors had this talent. Finding ancestors is rewarding. However, it's almost impossible to find out personal facts about them without having any written history or photos from other family members.

As I mentioned, my great-grandmother Annie had premonitions about things that would later come true, such as knowing she would not come back from a hospital stay. She died there.

I also shared my own experiences that started in childhood while living near a cemetery. These types of occurrences became more frequent as I got older.

When I was about eighteen years old, I saw my first ghost. This happened on a country road near where I was living at the time, outside of Milwaukee. I was driving with my sister on a two-lane highway with farm fields on either side of us. Suddenly, I noticed a man on a horse to the left of us in the field next to the car. He looked disheveled and was slumped in the saddle. He wasn't completely solid, he seemed translucent. I could see the outline of his body, his hat, old-fashioned clothing, and a canteen that was strapped to the saddle. I watched him as he approached on his horse, walking slowly through the field. He seemed not to notice anything around him and continued to ride into the road, right in front of my car. Even though I knew something wasn't normal about him, instinctively, I slammed on the brakes and the car came to a screeching halt. My sister asked, "What are you doing?" I told her I didn't want to hit the guy on the horse. She asked, "What guy?" I realized that I was the only one who could see him. Once I understood this, I was surprised, yet excited and wondered why I was able to have this experience.

After that, over the years, there were numerous happenings. When I was in my early twenties, on an overnight stay at an inn in Ohio, a ghost of a servant girl tried to push me down a flight of stairs. She came to me in a dream the night before. In the dream, she told me she died in her twenties during childbirth and was angry that I was able to live out my life as a young woman and she couldn't. The next morning, I was preparing to leave and started walking down a curved, narrow staircase to the kitchen that had been used by servants in the 1800s. I had an uneasy feeling in the close space. Then I felt a hand on my back and a light shove that made me lose my balance. Luckily there was a banister on the staircase that I grasped to steady myself. When I turned around no one was there. I felt it was the girl showing her dislike and she wanted me out of the house!

Other experiences include when I lived with my partner Joe in a haunted house that had a variety of ghosts; dreams that came true; a ghost dog that followed me down a garden path; spirits that showed up with smells that I strongly associate with them. One of which is my father, whose presence is announced by an overpowering smell of cigarette smoke, which I mentioned earlier. He was a heavy smoker in life. The smell is so strong at times that it makes me cough. My ex-father-in-law manifested after he died with delicious food smells. He owned a restaurant and created all the recipes from scratch. One day, I was in a back bedroom of my house and a strong smell of one his signature creations came into the room. No one was cooking and the kitchen was nowhere near the bedroom. I knew it was him coming to say hello.

Some of these experiences were a little scary, and some were welcome. Aunt Nan has strong psychic abilities. They aren't always positive, such as in the story I'm going to share now. Nan had a terrifying experience when her best friend Katie was murdered by her husband in 1980 when she was 29 years old. Katie had recently called Nan to let her know she was leaving her husband. He was living in Texas at the time and was coming back to Madison, Wisconsin where Katie lived, to pick up his stuff that weekend. She figured he'd pick up what he needed and go, so she made plans to travel to Milwaukee to meet Nan for fun that same weekend.

On Thursday night before Katie was due to arrive, Nan and her husband were sleeping in their bed, when in the middle of the night, Nan was awakened by the sound of the outside door shutting and footsteps coming up the stairs to their room. Nan tried to sit up, but she felt paralyzed and was unable to move or speak or wake up her husband. As the footsteps continued up the stairs, Nan was amazed their dog didn't respond to the noise and start barking. He was usually a great guard dog.

She heard the door open at the top of the stairs to their room and perceived a young man heading towards their bed. Even though she was trying to scream at the top of her lungs, no sound came out. The man, who was not totally visible in the dark, came right up to her side of the bed and aimed a gun at her temple. At that point, Nan could now physically scream, waking up her husband and the dog, but there was no intruder in the house. Was this just a bad nightmare? She was horribly upset by the event. She tried to shake it off.

Psychic Ancestry

A couple of days later, on Saturday morning, her phone rang. It was Katie's dad with the news that Katie had been murdered on Thursday night by her husband, who also killed himself and the family dog. She had been shot in the right temple at close range while sleeping in her bed. Nan psychically experienced the actions of the murder as it happened to Katie.

This is a very strong psychic experience. I'm glad nothing like this has happened to me. I'm not sure I could handle the emotion of it. This could have been an unintended "remote viewing." Remote viewing is when someone uses their psychic abilities to view and tune into what's happening to someone else who is at another location. One of the more popular examples of this was in the 1970s, when the U.S. government created the Stargate Project. The project, which lasted into the 1990s, was run by a secret Army unit that used psychics to "see" at a remote distance to gain intelligence for the CIA. There were many successes that came out of the project including finding a lost aircraft that belonged to the Soviet Union. A remote viewer was able to locate the plane and extract important information from it that led to its location. Even with some success, it was decided the program was not consistently accurate enough overall, so it ended. Yet there are rumors similar projects are still being used by world governments today.

I've done remote viewing exercises in classes and the results were surprising. In one exercise, I was able to describe specific rooms in an English country house I'd never been to.

Nan also had non-scary premonitions about a couple of future marriages, one being her own. After divorce, my grandmother Frances moved into a studio apartment. Nan was a young girl at the time and moved into the studio with her mom. On moving day, a man down the hall said hello to them as they were bringing boxes in. His name was Mr. Nelson. Nan started telling people Mr. Nelson was engaged to her mom, even though he was engaged to someone else at the time. This was news to Mr. Nelson! Nan's intuition proved to be right. Her mom, my grandmother, did eventually marry him.

Nan also knew she would marry her husband Frank before she met him. She was driving with a girlfriend and heard Frank on the radio. He was a disc jockey at WQFM, a popular radio station in Milwaukee. She thought he was hilarious and pulled over to the side of the road because she was laughing so hard. She told her friend, "I'm going to marry that guy." Interesting, since she didn't know him, but she loved it when she heard him on the radio. The next week, Nan needed help producing a public service announcement for work and called WQFM for help. The producer that helped her turned out to be Frank. She later married him, as she knew she would!

My mother had vivid experiences of traveling to other realms in her dreams. She didn't feel comfortable with this, so she shut it down as much as possible, but it would still happen on occasion, and she would tell me about it. She told me it was like traveling to other worlds and dimensions unlike earth. In all fairness, it could have been an effect of some of the drugs she was taking at the time for depression, but this cannot be confirmed.

And what about the men in the family? My great-grandfather Frederick's brother Frank Couper was a 32nd degree Freemason. He was one degree way from being a Scottish Rite Master Mason, a very high-ranking member. To be awarded their degrees, the Freemasons learn and perform theatrical rituals with storytelling about ancient mysteries. Their goings-on have a metaphysical and utopian vibe. They believe in a higher power and that all people are connected on a spiritual level. Each man aspires to learn and better himself. This may not mean Frank Couper possessed psychic skills, but he did have an inclination toward the magic and mystery surrounding the secret society of Freemasons.

Psychic Ancestry

Once again, I was hoping to uncover the reason I have psychic abilities and where it comes from in the family line. I do see evidence of it in the McIntosh family, which includes the women in Eliza's family line: Annie, Nan, my mother Barbara, and myself.

| Eliza (Black) Duncan Great, Great-Grandmother | → | Annie (McIntosh) Couper Great-Grandmother | → | Barbara Blair My Mother | → | Nan (Blair) Bialek My Aunt, (My Mom's Sister) | → | Terri Blair Me |

Eliza's family line simplified chart

That doesn't mean other ancestors didn't have these experiences. I simply hadn't found any evidence of it yet. I feared the psychic trail would end with me. I do not have children, and my only sister claims to have no psychic experiences, nor does her daughter. So, what then?

I decided to check with Nan's daughter, my cousin, Rebecca, to see if she's had any experiences. We made a date to meet for lunch to discuss this. A few days later, at a local pub, we had a revealing conversation. Rebecca said she had an interest in psychic happenings. She believes Nan's house, her childhood home, is haunted. When she was a child, a ghostly voice would whisper her name in her ear at night. Also, an unseen presence would lightly slap her face at bedtime. These were scary experiences, but she also had dreams that were unusual and didn't seem normal. In the dreams, she felt she was connecting to people in a psychic way through the dream experience. I think that if she wanted to pursue her own psychic abilities, she could easily develop her skills.

Rebecca also mentioned her younger brother, Ben, had a remarkable paranormal experience as a young child living in their house. Ben had an invisible friend named Charlie who visited him regularly. Here is Ben's story in his own words:

"I think that my parents bought our house in the summer of 1984 or 1985. So, thinking about it, I would have met Charlie right before my 3rd or 4th birthday. I remember our grandma driving us to our new home. I went into my bedroom and was happy to find my toys. That's when I first saw him, and he introduced himself as Charlie. I immediately told my parents and their friend Ed. They all said that there was nobody in my room and it was my imagination.

"Charlie had the shape of a man, dressed in clothes. I could never make out a face. To me the face was like a cloudy mirror. I asked him about it, and he told me it was because he was a shapeshifter who could change his form at will.

"Charlie always wore a red sweater with the image of a waterfall on it. To me that was him changing into an image I'd be comfortable with. The Care Bears cartoons were important to 3-year old me. All the Care Bears had different images on their tummies. The images were where the Care Bears got their strength to battle evil. Charlie said he derived his power from the water and having a water image on his bright sweater conveyed that to me without words. I wasn't sure of Charlie's age. He would present himself to me as a man who looked to be in his 30s. Part of him being a shapeshifter was that he could be any age or any thing.

"Charlie could range from being kind to terrifying. I tried talking to my parents about seeing him for a year or two, but my sister, and eventually, my grandma on my dad's side, Helen, were the only ones to take my word for it. I accepted that he was there. I went back and forth as to whether I thought he was a friend. Helen taught me a specific way to pray. She said that when you go to sleep the angels come to dance in your head and they aren't all good. She taught me to pray to be guided by the good angels. I took this to be a form of protection. The seemingly physical appearances of Charlie decreased in frequency, and by age seven, I never saw him again.

"Then a crazy thing happened, about thirty years later. Rebecca's four-year-old son Joseph, saw Charlie. He was visiting Nan's house and came out of Ben's old room saying he just talked to a ghost named Charlie. This sent chills down my spine and refreshed some repressed memories."

This is an amazing story from my cousin Ben! The water Charlie is referring to is Honey Creek, which runs underground in the neighborhood where Nan and her husband own their home. The same creek is directly across the street from the house I lived in, by the cemetery in my childhood. This is where I had the nightly hauntings that I attribute to the indigenous children buried under the street in front of the house.

Charlie's claim that his power was derived from water is also telling. It is theorized that spirits use the energy of water as a conduit to our world. Water is said to amplify spiritual energy. This may make it easier for ghosts and spirits to travel through liquids rather than solid objects. Energy in the form of electricity moves faster through water, so this could make sense.

Ben also shared with me that he experienced dream visions of his then nine-and ten-year old peers fighting in in the second Gulf War, about the time the first one began. The dreams were very specific about an attack that years later came to pass. Ben also had a vision that he would marry his wife, Emily. They dated when they were in middle school but broke up. After that, while traveling with his dad, he experienced a clear vision that he would be married to Emily. This happily did come to pass. Ben still has occasional visions. His wife Emily also has strong intuition. They are accepting of each other's abilities which creates a strong bond.

Learning about my two cousins' experiences makes me extremely happy. Most people would have this reaction after winning the lottery or if their favorite sports team won the championship. For me, finding out psychic abilities are alive and well in my family makes me feel fortunate. This means there is a continuation of the psychic nature of my ancestors. It also means I have living relatives who, like me, have had experiences and are open minded and are willing to share their stories.

Chapter 16
Protection

I was so excited when I realized I could use the mediumship techniques I was learning to ask my ancestors to participate in their own research, but I needed to ensure a good experience. My experience has been, asking for protection when practicing mediumship is necessary when communicating with someone in spirit. Both for myself and the person I'm connecting with.

For me, spirits don't manifest physically, I see them in my mind's eye. I can see what they look like, the clothes they're wearing and any objects or symbols they want to show me. When they communicate with words, it's done telepathically. When I begin a session, I always begin with a short ritual to set an intention for the reason I'm contacting a person on the other side, and to ask for protection plus express my gratitude to them.

I believe when we die, the energy of who we were in life still exists but on a different vibrational level. When I contact those who have passed on, I want to be sure I'm asking for only positive energy to come through. Ghosts, spirits, dead people, whatever you want to call them are still "people." I don't believe we become instantly enlightened or turn into saints when we die. As in life, some people are great, and some can be real jerks! So, I set up rules on how I want to be treated and how I will treat spirits.

Before beginning a session, I spend a few minutes being quiet and getting centered, and visualize a bright white protective light around myself and the person I want to contact. It's hard because I'm excited to get started and want to jump right in, but I think it's important to take a few minutes to set the intention that the exchange will be positive between the spirit and myself. I can end the session anytime if it doesn't feel good. When it's time to end the communication, and give closure to the session, I visualize them walking away surrounded by white light.

For example, a friend asked me to contact her maternal grandmother. As I tuned into her grandmother in a session, I could see she was bossy, and a complainer. I said to her telepathically "You must come with positive energy. Otherwise, I'll end the session now." She agreed to calm down and change her attitude, so we were able to continue with the reading.

Another time before I practiced protection regularly, I was caught off guard when a person I knew who died reached out to me unexpectedly. My friend James was brutally murdered in the late 1980s. He was a musician in my town, known for starting the punk rock movement in the area. As the front man for his band, he was a no-nonsense, tough guy who always looked cool and had a rebellious side to his personality. He was known for his honest nature, which sometimes got him in trouble with his friends. I knew James and his wife Maggie very well. We were even roommates for a time. We lived together in a charming but beat up historic house in an area that could be dangerous after dark.

Years later after he and his wife divorced, he lived in a similar neighborhood. One night as he walked alone on a deserted city street, three men approached him and demanded he give up his leather jacket. He refused, so they beat him to death. It was a violent and terrible end to his life.

About two years after his death, I had an unsettling experience. I was living in Phoenix, working full-time, and going to school five nights a week. With a full schedule like this, I really looked forward to a good night's sleep. One night around midnight, knocking on the wall behind my bed's headboard woke me up. The knocking persisted and I couldn't get back to sleep. I got up and looked everywhere in my apartment for the source of the knocking, but nothing was amiss. The knocking continued night after night, and I couldn't figure out where it was coming from. My downstairs neighbor who I knew well never heard a thing, and I believed him. I lived in a second-floor corner apartment so there was no one on the other side of the wall, just the neighbor below me.

A couple weeks into this, I had a dream. In the dream, James was standing on a bridge. He was on one side, and I was on the other. He said, "Please help me, I'm not happy here." I knew instantly he was manifesting his presence by knocking on my wall. In the spirit world, time isn't measured like it is here, so the event of his death was still very new to him. James knew I was into psychic practice and meditation, so like a light turned on in a dark hallway, he knew where to find me. Unfortunately, I was so upset and exhausted from sleepless nights, I had no clue how to help him. Luckily, a good friend of mine who worked as a medium in the area said she would try and help. She was able to connect with him and help him move on by showing him that he could work with people on the other side who had died suddenly, to help them process what had happened to them. It gave him a purpose in the afterlife. It took her several attempts, but he finally got it and the knocking stopped. She said, "He's excited to be helping others now," and was able to move forward.

At the time this was happening, I had no concept of "protection" from things like physical knocking. When meditating or reading Tarot cards, I always ask for the most benevolent outcome, but I wasn't prepared for the physical manifestation of noise. I needed to ask for help from someone more experienced than I was.

I've since learned to say no when I'm not comfortable and ask the spirit to move on or reach out to someone else for help. I think we always have the power to control the situation. One can tell the spirits to stop or go away. Although the situation with James seemed a bit scary and negative, it worked out very well in the end. He simply needed help and was able to get it.

Often a mediumship experience can be very helpful to the living. When my close friend Elfie's older sister died very unexpectedly, the cause of death was not determined. Elfie reached out to me to see if I could contact her sister to see if she was okay on the other side. Once in a meditative state, I asked for protection and called her sister in. I didn't know what she looked like since I'd never met her. The woman standing before me in my mind's eye was small and thin, with dark hair cut in a bob. She seemed worried that no one knew what happened to her. I asked her to tell me three things I did not know about her as evidence that I was connecting with the right person. She showed me a peach-colored silk scarf with gold threads running through it and a man's wide gold wedding band. She also mentioned that Elfie rode her old hand-me-down bike as a child. She also showed me that she was out dancing with an older gentleman on the other side. Lastly, she told me she was okay, and her death had been an accidental one, and most likely a bad reaction to some medication. She showed me an image to share with Elfie of a giant heart as a symbol of her love for her sister.

I called Elfie to see if any of these things were connected to her sister. She said "Yes!" The description of her appearance was accurate. A scarf and gold wedding band were in her sister's belongings that were collected from her apartment after she died. Her sister wasn't married, so the wedding band was a surprise, and no one knew who it belonged to. But it really doesn't matter who owned the ring, it was simply a piece of evidence that could be verified. Elfie also confirmed that when she was a kid, she did ride the hand-me-down bike. Elfie's family is large, and she has many siblings, but the bike was this particular sister's bike. Her sister also liked to go dancing with an older male friend. The image of the big heart, along with all the evidence, comforted Elfie. Even though the cause of death couldn't be confirmed, she felt certain her sister was doing well in the afterlife.

A simpler, less precise technique commonly used to contact spirits is a Ouija Board. I think people should be a little careful of Ouija Boards. Using it can lack direction and leave one open to unwanted entities and the riffraff of the spirit world. I've used Ouija boards but always ask for protection first and that only spirits with good intentions connect using this method. It can be fun to see what answers you get to your questions. My friend and I have a routine on Mother's Day. Both our mothers have passed on, so we like to check in with them once a year using the board. The messages we get are always pretty good, and in the exact words our mothers would have used. But once again, protection first!

I think people who do any kind of psychic work are highly sensitive. I grew up with unusual happenings starting at an early age. Because my parents were heavy drinkers and smokers, I was very tuned into them on a psychic level and intuitively felt I needed to protect myself and my siblings from their energy. They would often go to bed and leave multiple lit cigarettes. Sometimes a cigarette would be left on the edge of a wood table, not in an ashtray, but burning directly on the furniture. I would make myself stay up until they were asleep and then go around the house and put out all the cigarettes so there wasn't a fire. This type of thing made me hyper vigilant and fine-tuned my intuition at a young age. My intuition was a form of protection against danger.

To sum up, I think of psychic protection in the same way as wearing a seatbelt in a car or a life jacket when paddling a canoe. It's a quick and easy step to ensure safety when connecting with spirits. Mediumship has given me rich, positive, and rewarding experiences. I feel a genuine connection to the people and ancestors I've met with in spirit and feel this is a valuable tool in my research. A little extra step is well worth the effort.

Along with our own protective efforts, I believe the spirit world helps us in ways that can be surprising. I will talk about some ways this can happen in the next chapter.

Chapter 17
Spirit Guides & Guardian Angels

It's a perfectly natural occurrence to have guides and helpers who aren't of the earthly domain. I believe we all have spirit guides and guardian angels. Many different religions and cultures subscribe to the belief in spirit guides and guardian angels of some sort. Most of Christianity, Judaism and Islam hold that every person has one. They are said to surround each of us with their watchful care and help us when we need it. Throughout the world, ancestors are also revered. They are honored and called upon for assistance in our daily lives.

Spirit guides are said to reside in the spiritual realm and make their wisdom and protection available to us. Guides can help by giving us practical information and guidance. They assist in our daily lives whether one is aware of it or not. It is said that people often have one main guide but may also have many different guides throughout their lifetime.

Examples of spiritual entities that can work with us include ancestors, departed loved ones, guardian angels, archangels, ascended masters, deities, and animal helpers. Spirit guides may have existed in human form at one time or were never incarnated but are energetic beings that want to assist us. Ascended masters are teachers who watch over us from the spiritual world. They may inspire us through their teachings. A deity is a supernatural being who is divine in nature. For instance, one Scottish deity is Druantia. She represents fertility, passion, sex, trees, protection, knowledge, and creativity. She covers lots of topics!

How do these beings show up for us? For me, mostly they have shown up via clairvoyance, which means I perceive them visually in my mind's eye. Some people "feel" their presence, which would be clairsentience. When doing mediumship, I can sometimes feel the spirit I'm connecting with standing near me. Or with clairaudience I may hear a sound, voice, song, or other noise that is a connection. A few times in my life, I believe my mom communicated by sending a certain song to me. She loved country music, especially Roger Miller. If I hear the song "King of the Road" in some obscure place that wouldn't normally play that music, I feel it's her sending me a message.

One can call on guides and helpers when in need of clarity about a situation, needing motivation or for guidance when feeling stuck. What is meant by "call on" is to request their help. A person can do this in a meditation or by sitting quietly and imagining a connection with a guide of choice. Writing out a question is another way to connect with guides. By focusing on the question, and writing down what comes to mind, it can open a person to guidance. It's important not to judge, just write. It's amazing the insights that are revealed this way.

I became aware of my spirit guides through meditation when I was in my forties. In a psychic development class, I was told we all have guides and could meet them anytime we want. I could ask for them. This was intriguing and I wanted to know more. I didn't meet them all at the same time, but several years apart. They showed up when I was in need and ready for them to reveal their presence.

After falling and shattering my wrist, I needed surgery. As the anesthesiologist was putting me under, a white and brown spotted cat showed up in my mind's eye. The cat was sitting and looking at me. It seemed like a protector and a feeling of comfort came over me. The surgery went better than expected, and I didn't need a metal pin inserted as my surgeon originally predicted. This may have been an animal guide.

I have a few spirit guides. One of my recent guides is named Ivan, whom I've mentioned earlier. He lives in New Orleans in a home on St Charles Avenue. He's a handsome man, with dark curly hair, dressed in black pants and matching vest with a white lacy shirt underneath, open at the neck. A single silver earring hangs from one ear. His house is decorated with beautiful furniture and artwork. There's a marble fireplace and candles everywhere. And of course, he has his glass of sherry on a table next to him.

I met Ivan clairvoyantly during a meditation. I recognized his surroundings as New Orleans since I've visited there many times. He introduced himself as someone who is here to help me with mediumship. I liked him immediately. He's funny in a sarcastic way, but also kind. I've called on him to join in during mediumship training to help me get clear messages from the spirits. When I request his presence, there is greater detail with the images I see.

Years earlier, in a seminar in Sedona, Arizona, led by the late Richard Sutphen, in a group meditation we were told we would meet one of our guides. My curiosity was high. What would my spirit guide be like? Would he be an old man with a long white beard, grizzled and wise? Or would my guide be a woman? I was excited to find out. As I closed my eyes and began to meditate, a person started to come into view. It was a man who looked to be in his 30s. His dark hair was long and straight. He was strong and capable. He had a tribal feel, and wasn't wearing much clothing then, but has since shown himself in t-shirts, jeans, boots, and simple jewelry, like a polished stone necklace. He also has some great sunglasses. He told me he is my main spirit guide and had been with me all along.

I was happy to meet him while visiting the Southwest, where I had lived for a few years. I've always had an affinity for the land and the Native American culture and still travel there often.

This spirit guide helped me calm down in several situations. I've also asked him for advice about personal matters and he's shown me solutions. These solutions come in the form of images and visions. He is always available if I need to call on him. I've also asked him to show me signs that I'm on the right track with something. For instance, I asked him to send me a large feather as a confirmation about a certain situation. Out walking that same day, a large white feather showed up on the sidewalk in front of me. This is a physical manifestation of his confirmation.

When I was going through a divorce, I met a new female guide. Like my other guides, I became aware of her during a meditation. She was a fierce-looking woman, like the warrior women of the ancient world. She had weapons. She liked knives. She always seemed to be holding one. Her name was something I couldn't pronounce, so she said I could call her Polly. That name didn't exactly match her looks, but it was easy for me to remember. There were many times I called on her during my divorce process. My soon-to-be ex-husband would sometimes make threats and leave me nasty notes at my apartment. If I felt threatened, I would call on her to be with me. She was not going to let anything happen to me or let him come close. She stayed with me until the divorce was final and then she began to fade away. I felt a strong protective sensation when she was near.

In addition to my spirit guides, I have another helper in the form of a guardian angel. At least, that's how I think of him. This guide or angel is a physical being, not a spirit. Starting at a young age, this man showed up in my life in times of personal danger. He wears a fedora. That's how I recognize him. The first time he helped me was when I was about seven years old.

As a quiet, shy girl growing up in a turbulent household, I didn't have many friends. When the most popular girl in the neighborhood asked me to come outside to play, I was excited. She was also a bully. She called me over to opposite side of the street from my house. Once we were together, instead of playing, she started pushing me around and hitting me. I was a small kid, and she could have beat me up easily. This caught me off guard, and I didn't know what to do. She continued to rough me up. Then a car pulled up alongside of us.

The man driving was wearing a suit and a fedora. He got out of his car. At the sight of him, the girl stopped her attack and ran home. For some reason, I felt I could trust this man. He then watched to make sure I made it back to my house safely. My feelings were more hurt than anything. I thought the girl liked me and wanted to play. At the time, I was thankful, but didn't think too much about the nice man in the hat.

Years later, when I was in my late teens, I took the city bus across town to attend an event. Mistakenly, I got on the wrong bus. I didn't realize my error until we started to drive through some dangerous parts of town. Even bus drivers were afraid to drive this route as there had been many armed robberies on buses. At one point, the bus made a stop on a corner and picked up an elderly man. He looked frail and wore a suit and a fedora. He boarded the bus and without making eye contact, walked down the aisle, and sat down in the empty seat next to me. I felt instantly safe, even though this man could not have defended me. He stared straight ahead and never said a word.

Once the bus passed the dangerous neighborhoods, he got up and left. When I reached my destination, the bus driver said to me, "I was really worried about you. You never should have been on this bus, it's not safe." For the first time, I knew the man in the hat was a protector and got me safely through a difficult situation.

This guardian angel manifested in human form which is different than my spirit guides. My guides appear to me by use of my inner vision. It made me wonder if guardian angels simply manifest in the flesh as apparent humans, or if they are real humans assigned to protect us. I'm not sure I have that answer, but I will tell you mine is very real. I never questioned it. I allowed this angel into my life. My spirit guides are in my thoughts and meditations daily, but my guardian angel appeared in real life when needed.

It could be a coincidence that an older man in a fedora came to my rescue twice. But four times? It was Christmas Eve sometime in the early 80s, and a big snowstorm was forecasted for that night. At the time, I was in my 20s, living in a new apartment complex west of Milwaukee. It was outside of the city limits, so I used a few country roads to get back and forth to my job in the city. I was looking forward to my family coming over later that night to celebrate and check out my new place.

It was about dusk and snowing lightly as I headed home from work. As I got closer to my apartment, the storm intensified, and the snow started coming down hard. It was difficult to see the road ahead once I got onto the country roads. There were no streetlights and nothing but woods on either side of me. However, I had faith my trusty old Honda Civic would get me home safely.

Suddenly, my car started slowing down for no apparent reason. I was able to pull over to the side of the road, but the engine went completely dead, and wouldn't start again. Oh no! I had people coming over and there were no houses or businesses on the lonely road. This was long before winter tech gear or cell phones. I was wearing my useless but fashionable black coat and non-winter type boots. There was no way I could hike the couple of miles to my apartment.

At this point, I started crying, feeling I was doomed. Five minutes later, I noticed car headlights approaching on the road behind me. The car slowed down and pulled up next to me. It was a local pizza delivery car, with a glowing "Ned's Pizza" sign on the roof. The driver was an older man, wearing a fedora and black overcoat. He rolled down his window and asked if I needed help.

I like to think of myself as being streetwise, so normally, I would have ignored him and locked the car doors. But for some reason, I felt strangely comforted and accepted his offer of a ride. I looked inside his car, and on the front seat, sat a pizza-warming container, so I felt he was legit. He moved it aside and said, "Come on in." I got in and told him where I needed to go. I asked him why he was delivering pizza this late on Christmas Eve in the middle of a blizzard. He just smiled and didn't say anything. It was a quiet ride to my apartment, and we rolled up without incident. I thanked him profusely, tried to give him a tip, which he refused, and wished him a Merry Christmas as he drove off.

I would need to call a tow truck to get my car after the holiday, but I was so relieved to be home. I arrived at my apartment in plenty of time to get ready for my guests, who eventually made it over as the storm tapered off.

The day after Christmas, I called Ned's Pizza to tell the manager how grateful I was that their driver stopped and helped me that night. The manager was surprised since the restaurant was not open on Christmas Eve and no one matching the man's description worked there or ever did. Someone drove me home that night and I don't think it was someone impersonating a pizza delivery driver. I'm forever thankful.

Since 1995, I have only seen the man in the fedora one other time. After living in Phoenix for five years, I decided to try Florida for a while. It was time to move on from Arizona, but I wasn't ready to move back to the Midwest quite yet.

It was a long, lonely drive from Phoenix, down through New Mexico, Texas, and other states to get to Miami. Once there, I looked for work, but the job market was terrible. No luck finding a job. Friends of mine lived in Jacksonville, so I thought I would try to find work there. I did find a job as a graphic artist creating artwork for military training videos. It was a fun job, but the pay was low.

After about a year, hot humid weather, cockroaches, and a failed relationship made me throw in the towel. The cost of living was high, and my apartment was expensive. I thought it was best to pack up and head back to my hometown to regroup for a while. After saying goodbye to my friends and co-workers, I hit the road. My first stop from Jacksonville was St. Simons Island, Georgia. A friend of mine invited me to stay for a few days on my way north.

As I started my drive, I was overwhelmed with sadness and a sense of failure. My job in Phoenix ended abruptly, and now I couldn't make it work in Florida. The last thing I wanted was to move back to the cold, damp climate of Wisconsin. Even though I was happy with my job in Jacksonville, there was no opportunity for advancement. So the time was right to leave.

The highway, full of potholes, stretched out in both directions. Flat land and hot sun. I pointed my car in the direction of Georgia and started my journey. I only got about five miles into my drive when I started crying uncontrollably. I just kept driving. An older model car pulled in front of me on the road and was going pretty slow. It didn't bother me since my eyes were blurry and going fast was not an option at the moment. In a while, I calmed down and accepted my fate. I was going back to Milwaukee.

As my eyes began to focus better, I noticed the man in the fedora behind the wheel of the old car. I knew who he was. He stayed ahead of me for miles and escorted me to the border of Florida and Georgia, then drove off in another direction. I never learned the man's name, and almost never heard him speak, but I will recognize him, if he shows up in my life again.

I made it back to the Midwest and I've stayed here ever since. Life has become quite wonderful. If I'd stayed in Florida, my life would have been very different. It was the right move.

To have spirit guides helping me now with mediumship is something I never expected. How do I know if these helpers are real? I don't. But, I've been guided and helped in my life when I really needed it from beyond.

Part Six
How I Did It & Epilogue

Chapter 18
How I Did It & Sometimes Things Just Show Up

If I never investigated my ancestors or learned mediumship, I'm sure my life would have moved along just fine. Instead, with these new experiences, my world expanded in a huge way. I felt like I was traveling back in time to places my ancestors lived, worked, and died. It was a vivid experience, especially because I met some of them in spirit. I will never forget how they looked, the clothes they were wearing, or the whiff of pipe tobacco that came out of nowhere.

Ancestry research takes a ton of patience, perseverance, time, and luck. For me, it was worth the effort. Often, I would sit down at my computer to look up one thing and realize several hours had passed. It was addicting. I had no idea how much broader my life would become as I got to know the people in my family who came before me. I wrote the stories of my ancestors in real time, as I was researching them, and learning mediumship. It was exciting because I never knew what was around the next corner. And what might show up.

The stories I uncovered, from pirates and sea captains, to pioneers, enslavers, and Wisconsin families, are fascinating. Many, and perhaps most, people are interested in their ancestors. As humans, it's natural to want to know where we come from. When I began my research, I had no idea where to start, but I jumped right in to look for Eliza and her daughter, Annie MacIntosh, with Familysearch.org, which is a free service. Later, the process evolved to include a variety of sources, some free and some paid.

The techniques I used were a mix of psychic skills and conventional research. Traditional sources included ancestry websites, birth, death and census records, tax rolls, wills, passenger manifests, plat maps, historical references, interviews with living relatives, family stories, photos, memories and written letters, historical societies, and visits to cemeteries and courthouses. Non-traditional methods included psychic impressions, intuition, spirit guides, automatic writing, and mediumship. I also subscribed to a few Scottish podcasts about folklore and witchcraft.

Mediumship brought a unique element to this research. There was something about talking to my deceased ancestors that worked. I felt if I was sincere in my approach to telling their stories, that they would guide me. And many did. I was willing to believe them and to listen and to watch for subtle clues and nudges. Often, if I was heading down the wrong research path, I would get a strong feeling that something wasn't right. This could be my intuition, which I have learned to trust, but it could also be an ancestor urging me to look again, dig deeper, or start over completely with their story. If I were going to tell their story, they wanted me to get it right.

Some of the spirits that came through for me were the movie star Hedy Lamarr, my friend's uncle, Oscar Zerk, my mother, my grandfather Sylvon, my grandmother Julia, George's alleged father (name unknown), my great-grandmother Annie and her mother Eliza, Frank Couper, William Santas, and my ancestors from the Scottish Highlands.

Understandably, not everyone will want to learn mediumship to talk to their ancestors, but other mediums can help. For example, in a mediumship session, a medium connected with my grandfather Sylvon and his dog Johann to bring me a message. Also, the spirit of William Santas came through a fellow mediumship student in Wonewoc, to let me know he was around.

The William Santas story is a good example of a nudge from beyond. For over a year, following data from ancestry.com, I built his family tree with false information. I thought he was a descendant of a prominent German family in Pennsylvania, and he was not. As I was compiling the data, I felt intuitively something was wrong. I couldn't find any evidence that William was tied to this family even though the website said he was. Then I visited Wonewoc, Wisconsin, and William's grave, and everything changed. Joe and I felt compelled to investigate a road that "showed up" on the car navigation system even though we weren't near it. The road was Santas Loop. The same road that members of the Santas family have lived along for generations. This nudge put me on the right path to learn the correct history of my ancestors in Wisconsin. It would have been nice if this happened sooner in the process, however.

Was there a spirit who prodded the lady at the Mauston Historical Society to tell me about Wonewoc Spiritualist Camp? She told me about it as I was preparing to leave after spending two hours with her. I wondered if this was by chance. Perhaps she was a channel for another energy. She had never been there herself. Whatever the reason, this was serendipity, and I'm very grateful for it. The spiritualist camp has become an important part of my life.

Automatic writing gave me another way to communicate. I don't remember exactly when I learned about automatic writing, but it was in one of my psychic development classes when I was in my thirties. This method became popular during the spiritualism craze in the U.S. and Europe during the 19th century. While not foolproof, it was a fun way to connect with ancestors. The few times I used this process, I got some unexpected results. The spirit named Mary, who was probably a contemporary of the women in the photo of the four Couper women, messed with me a bit, and my Highland women ancestors gave me a special insight into their lives.

Traditional research methods, such as the well-kept Scottish birth and death records on scotlandspeople.gov.uk, were a great resource. They are a wealth of information. The records are clearly written with beautiful penmanship, although some of the letters needed a bit of deciphering. When my ancestor Eliza gave me the name of Jimmy during a mediumship session, at first, I was baffled. Who could this be? But with the help of birth and census records, I was able to figure out that James McIntosh, the brother of the man that raised my great-grandmother Annie, was her real father.

Scottish death records are especially helpful. They show the name of the deceased and their parents, including the maiden name of the mother. This was important in verifying if ancestry.com had the correct parents for a particular person, although sometimes it was incorrect on the website. The Scottish record also shows if the deceased was born out of wedlock (illegitimate). This enabled me to look for the father of a person if their name was not listed on the birth record or death record. It also shows date, time, and cause of death. The place where the person died is noted, along with the last known address of the person and a family member as witness.

This is one way I was able to confirm that Thomas Smith Couper was the same person as the obituary in the Dundee newspaper, even though many details of his life were missing. He was listed as living on Thistle Street in Falkirk on his death record and the obituary. The death record has his correct parents and other verifiable information.

I found that popular ancestry sites sometimes have the wrong information. This could be because another person who is building a family tree added wrong data, which is then circulated by the program. That's why it was important for me to seek and compare multiple sources. And even then, I made mistakes, such as Poorhouse Alexandrina.

Wills are accessible on many of the ancestry websites. I found the will of John Blair, where I learned about the sale of his enslaved people upon his death. Also, the will of William Couper, which gave details on the amount of money he had when he died and who he left it to. And the story of the only possession he left to anyone, a watch, to his grandson, George Couper.

Census records helped me to track where people lived, how often they moved, the names of wives, husbands, and children. By reviewing census records, I was able to determine the names of children who didn't live to adulthood. In my family's written history, the names of children who died young were not recorded. Sad, but true. On a census record for Jane Hay, it was confirmed that Annie McIntosh was her granddaughter. This was an important finding.

On Findagrave.com, I found many photos of my ancestor's gravestones. Headstones often have details on them I didn't expect to find. On this site, I also searched by cemetery in a village or town. This was helpful to find other ancestors other than the one I was looking for. Often on a page for one ancestor, I found several other family members listed with photos of them or their gravesites. I loved to look at the old grave markers. Often they are decorative, and look aged and a little creepy.

Historical societies both in person and online have been a good resource for me. The Tulsa, Oklahoma Historical Society found pictures of Frank Couper's surgical supply company. I simply called them up. An old-fashioned way of communicating! The gentleman who answered the phone was most helpful. I've had good and bad experiences with small town historical societies, but it's worth spending the money for a couple of hours of research. Usually they charge by the hour, so I limited the time to two hours initially, and if they found information, I added additional hours. Occasionally, I got lucky, and the help was free.

Photos helped fill out the stories of my ancestors. When I found the old portrait style picture of what turned out to be the four Alexandrinas, I was curious about who these women were. I knew they were in the Couper family, but I had no idea who was who in the photo. When the photo went missing at Nan's house, I found a smaller version of it months later. Names were listed on the back. The original photo has never resurfaced. It was a large picture, so it should be easy to find. However, strange things do happen in Nan's house. The spoon fell off the wall display in her hallway the day I contacted my great-grandmother Annie through mediumship. And the ghost named Charlie still seems to reside there.

Newspapers.com and British Newspaper Archives were another resource. This took patience! When I typed in an exact name in the search bar, often nothing came up. When I typed the same name in the "contains these words" search bar, I found all kinds of related articles about my ancestors. It just took longer, since I had to weed through several people with the same first name, then the last name to find anything. This is where the glass of wine next to my computer came in. Sip, search, look, and look again. One day, the obituary of Thomas Smith Couper simply "showed up" after I searched for it numerous times in the exact same way. Spirit assistance perhaps, or interference.

Newspapers give an insight into the life of a town or village. It was easy to get sidetracked reading articles and ads in the papers about all kinds of things. I found one about a woman in Dundee in the 1800s, complete with photos, who lived as a man for many years. She eventually revealed she was a woman. This was a scandal at the time, although in today's world it would not be news. I got a feel for the local politics, social scene, human interest stories and more. This is how I discovered the story of Sandy-No-More, the wanderer in the Highlands.

Ship manifests documented when my ancestors came to America, their country of origin, who they knew in the United States, where they planned to go once they arrived, and sometimes age and physical descriptions. Because many of the Couper's physical characteristics were listed on the manifests, I could imagine what they looked like. I don't have photos of everyone. Finding out that all the Coupers were 5'4" or under made me feel like I fit right into the family line! I'm still amazed at how brave they all were, to travel by ship and start over in a new country.

Old books were helpful. I found one book written in 1932 called *The Pageant of Morayland* about local history of Elgin and Moray County. It was fascinating. I had no idea the national animal of Scotland is a unicorn! This book is full of local legend about royalty, castles, clans, battles, mythology, witchcraft and more. Another helpful book called *DP & L* was written about the sailing and ship-building history of Dundee, Scotland. This book included a list of all the Dundee shipowners along with ship names, their histories, and photos. Internet research is helpful, but reading an entire book about shipbuilding really gave me a rich picture of the life of my sea captain ancestors.

Interviewing family members was eye-opening. Nan told the wild story about her best friend Katie's murder, and how she witnessed it remotely in real time. Also, Nan's kids had their own stories to tell. When my cousins, Rebecca and Ben, were growing up, I didn't see them much. As I was writing about other family members who may have psychic abilities, it dawned on me to ask them. At lunch, when Rebecca told me about Ben and the ghost named Charlie, I immediately got in touch with Ben. He was living away from me, in Denver at the time, so through emails and phone calls, I heard the story of this childhood ghost.

Researching and connecting with my departed ancestors is by far one of the most fun things I've ever done. Although there were times I cursed at the computer after hours of research with nothing to show for it. Some of my ancestors were willing to communicate with me and others were not, at least not yet. I was really hoping to get in touch with my ancestor, Fannie Syrene Blair. I was born on her birthday, 100 years later. But I didn't have any luck. I tried several times and nothing. I am happy for the times I was able to speak with my ancestors intuitively, some with the help of my spirit guide, Ivan.

One of the hardest parts of writing my stories was talking about myself. It proved to be a lot more difficult than I thought. A friend and writing coach would often say, "You need to add more of yourself to the story." I would cringe and think, really? I didn't always feel like doing that. However, this is my story along with that of my ancestors, and there was much to tell. This was a life-changing journey for me because I had to pull stories out my own past. And reveal things I've never told to anyone.

I realize I don't give step-by-step instructions in the book about how to use the paranormal to connect with ancestors. This kind of information and guidance can be found from many other sources. But I will say, it takes practice. Most important of all is learning how to sharpen and trust one's intuition.

As I was nearing the end of my research, a friend recommended a book called *Psychic Roots*, written by Henry (Hank) Z. Jones in 1993. Hank was a successful Hollywood actor who gave up his career to become a full-time genealogist. In developing his book, he invited professional genealogists to send him stories about how they solved ancestor mysteries by coincidence, unexplained events, serendipity, hunches, and intuition. And in his case, he writes about what he called his own preternatural experiences, including some help from the other side. He had such a big response to his query to genealogists about their non-traditional methods that he wrote a sequel to the first book!

How I Did It & Sometimes Things Just Show Up

After reading *Psychic Roots*, I was so excited that I was not alone in my psychic approach to ancestry that I immediately sent Hank an email. At the time I contacted him, he was 83 years old and retired from writing, but he responded. He was very encouraging and wished me well and "good hunting." And good hunting it has been. And as Hank might say, "with a little bit of the Twilight Zone" thrown in there.

Example of Scottish death record for Angus McIntosh

Epilogue

As I close, I will share some final thoughts about what I learned in the process of writing this book.

After researching my ancestry, I began to understand the wide range of my own heritage. My work has created a rich backdrop to my life, and there is a lot to absorb. Many of the skills and talents of my ancestors live on in me. In my ancestral DNA. Knowing this, my life can never be the same, and I am glad for it. It took many years to learn what I learned, and it was emotional at times. When I started, I knew the names of my grandparents and the countries where their parents were born. And not much else about the family members who came before. I hope my discoveries spark an interest in you to search for your own ancestors.

On the psychic side, mediumship was new to me, even though I have established psychic skills. I was learning it at the same time as I was doing my research. I was struck by how cool and inspiring it is. This brought the unexpected and proved to be very insightful. In the beginning, I started out with mediumship as a curiosity, and an additional skill. But as I progressed in my studies, I came to know it as a valuable way to comfort people and connect them with their loved ones who have passed on. And like other psychic skills, it is an incredible tool for ancestry and discovery. I also realized I gave my ancestors an opening to reach across the veil and talk to me.

I encourage you to explore your own psychic potential. It's important to say that anyone in our world can do this. However, there can be fear around the paranormal. Or there can be great interest. I've seen participants at psychic seminars who have never had a psychic experience give accurate readings for other people with seemingly no effort, once they put their fear aside. It's real and everyone has access to this age-old human ability.

Another wonderful thing that came out of writing these stories is that it brought me closer to my own living family members, as strange as they think I am sometimes. I also met new ones, such as the Santas family in Wisconsin. In knowing about the lives of my ancestors my life is fuller than it was before. I feel them walking along side me in spirit.

Resources

Psychic & Mediumship Development:

Edgar Cayce Association of Research and Enlightenment. (A.R.E.)
Edgarcayce.org
In-person and online classes
With a membership: Access to the Cayce readings

Sacredmessages.com
Richard P. Scholler-Medium & Teacher
Sign up for his newsletter or book a reading.

Spiritualist Camps in the U.S.
https://sunsetcamp.org/us-spiritualist-camp-directory/

The Shift Network
Theshiftnetwork.com
Online resource for psychic and mediumship training

The Society for Psychical Research (SPR)
https://www.spr.ac.uk/
In-person and online classes (UK)

Ions/Noetic Sciences
Noetic.org
In-person and online classes (U.S.)
Neuroscience, Philosophy and Mysticism

The Sir Arthur Conan Doyle Centre
Arthurconandolyecentre.com
In-person and online classes (Scotland)

Ancestry Research:

Ancestry.com
Subscription service for ancestry research

Familysearch.org
Free resource from the LDS Church

Scotlandspeople.gov.uk
Excellent resource for Scottish ancestry. Charges a small fee for downloading documents.

Ellis Island Foundation
www.libertyellisfoundation.org/passenger
Passenger and ship search capabilities

Find a Grave
Findagrave.com
Lookup graves, people, and memorials, photos, and cemeteries.

BillionGraves
Billiongraves.com
Lookup graves, people, and memorials, photos, and cemeteries with GPS information.

Newspaper Articles and Listings
Newspapers.com
Subscription service

British Newspaper Archive
Britishnewspaperarchive.co.uk
You can purchase several downloads at a time at a reasonable cost.

Find My Past (UK-based)
Findmypast.com
Subscription service

Resources

National Archives (Ships)
www.archives.com
Look up ships, crews and captains and military records.

Historical Societies
In general, always a great resource. Look up by searching the area or town you want to research. They will have various ways of contacting them to help with your research.

Books on Meditation, Spiritualism, and Mediumship

Creative Visualization by Shakti Gawain. Publisher: New World Library, 2016

Meditations for Psychic Development: Practical Exercises to Awaken Your Sixth Sense by Chanda Parkinson. Publisher: Llewellyn, 2021

The Beginners Guide to Mediumship by Larry Dreller. Publisher: Weiser Books, 1997

Edgar Cayce's Story of the Soul by W.H. Church. Publisher: A.R.E. Press, 1991

Lily Dale, The True Story of the Town that Talks to the Dead by Christine Wicker. Publisher: Harper San Francisco, 2003

The Reluctant Spiritualist, the Life of Maggie Fox by Nancy Rubin Stuart. Publisher: Houghten Miftlin Harcourt, 2005

Talking to the Other Side: A History of Modern Spiritualism by Todd Jay Leonard, Ph.D. Publisher: iUniverse Books, 2005

The Afterlife Frequency by Mark Anthony. Publisher: New World Library, 2021

Mediumship-Sacred Communication with Loved Ones Across the Veil by Suzanne Geisemann. Publisher: Sacred Stories Publishing, 2024

www.ingramcontent.com/pod-product-compliance
Lightning Source LLC
Chambersburg PA
CBHW060501030426
42337CB00015B/1684